Cubism, Stieglitz, and the Early Poetry of William Carlos Williams

"These are the hieroglyphics of a new speech between those of us who find all the spoken languages too clumsy."

—EGMONT ARENS

Cubism, Stieglitz, and the Early Poetry of William Carlos Williams

Bram Dijkstra

Princeton University Press
Princeton, New Jersey

FOR SANDRA
OF COURSE

PREFACE

"Every twenty years or so," William Carlos Williams once wrote to Alfred Stieglitz, "the boys have to be brought up short because of what they've forgot." If the artist himself often has difficulty remembering the goals he has set, how easy is it for those who attempt to reconstruct the artist's initial intentions to emphasize only those features of his development which he has allowed himself to remember, or which fit readily into the critic's own frame of reference.

This book attempts to discuss the early years of Williams' creative activity partly by means of what the poet remembered, and partly by reconstructing the elements of influence which determined the structure of his work during his formative years, but which he later came to, or perhaps wanted to, forget. In Williams' case such an attempt at reconstruction leads inevitably to the realm of the visual arts, to the world of those artists who, during the early years of this century, created a tightly knit and very adventurous avant garde community in New York, and there set out to develop the implications of such Parisian discoveries as Cubism and "Simultaneism."

Literature and the visual arts have always been very closely related. No one would deny that often their stylistic development has been remarkably parallel. It has, indeed, become customary to use terms borrowed from art history to classify or describe certain novels or poems. But it is curious that while these general thematic or structural resemblances are taken for granted, most people seem to assume that such similarities are primarily due to the common influence exerted on both writers and painters by the general temper of their period. It is considered perfectly legitimate to point to the influence of one writer on another, or the debt of one painter to another, but few people, apparently, accept the notion that painters and poets might have had an immediate formative influence on each other, that the structure and content of a writer's work might have been influenced quite directly by specific paintings, or a specific style of painting. Comparative studies of reciprocal influences between various literatures are becoming quite common, but the connections between literature and the visual arts are almost never approached from this view, even though many writers have openly shown a singular fascination for certain structural developments in painting, or for the works of specific painters.

Perhaps such reluctance is due to the fact that while the artistic mind, more often than not, is expansive and almost indiscriminately receptive to possibilities, the scholar's attitude is likely to be reductive, and narrowly focused. The critic, after all, tends to judge, to evaluate the works he is concerned with, according to a personal set of generalized positives and negatives whose range, unfortunately, is limited to the bounds of his own knowledge. The artist, on the other hand, while in certain respects not any less hoodwinked than the scholar, usually takes the whole field of the creative imagination, in all its disparate forms, as proper material for the construction of his own method of expression.

As a consequence, a work of literature whose form and content may have been determined at least in part by its author's attempts to emulate the achievements of another art is likely to be discussed and analyzed by scholars who are unprepared to deal with influences which do not originate within literature itself. Too often writing is regarded as an inherently self-contained act of verbal consciousness. Too often it is taken for granted that in his stylistic or conceptual development a writer will make use only of the literary tradition with which he is familiar, or that he will show in his work the influence of only those cultural themes of his day which are contained in verbal experience. It is assumed that he suffers from an occupational limitation which makes him unable to adapt to his own use those innovations which have revolutionized another form of artistic expression.

The poetry of William Carlos Williams has generally been approached in just such a manner. Few have been willing to assume that he meant what he said when he remarked that "a poet should take his inspiration from the other arts too." When he emphasized that the French poets had had virtually no influence on his poetry, but that French painting had been of major importance to his development, the response from a critic was that he had "overstated the case for the painters." If one surveys Williams criticism it becomes clear that the relationship of his work to the visual arts has been largely ignored, or has been approached in a very summary fashion and with great awkwardness. Most often Williams' intense fascination with painting has been dismissed as "of minor importance." The ability of some literary scholars to deal with other arts can be exemplified by the case of one who assumed, when Williams told him that Böcklin's "Insel des Todes" had affected him while he was writing a certain early work, that the poet must have *read* this work while studying in Germany.

There is no easy way to deal with the range of interests which may have helped to determine the ultimate character of an artist's work. The real developments, the innovations, in art and life, whether in literature or painting, depend on the manner in which the elements of one medium are translated to the conditions of another. Thus, if an artist's work is strikingly different from that of his predecessors or contemporaries, one may well look for the source of his originality to those of his interests which fall outside the proper sphere of his own medium. If the innovations current in one art are so striking that they make headlines in the daily press and cause waves of controversy, it is foolish not to look for repercussions in the work of the exponents of the new in other media. Ultimately, then, the arts depend for their development on the intelligent synthesizing capacities and free-ranging imagination of a few artists exceptionally attuned to the possibilities implicit in the texture of structural alternatives offered by the media of expression in their time. The innovations of such artists, therefore, small as they may seem when reexamined from a point in time when they have become common form, have an initial impact on the artistic movements of *their* time which cannot be exaggerated. Often their influence is ultimately greatest among those who were at first tempted to reject or dismiss these innovations as insignificant, fraudulent, or insane. A single painting, a single gesture of contempt or affirmation, a single poem, if it is an invention in the true sense, can do more to subvert established conventions and redirect the creative mind than the whole oeuvre of a brilliant but essentially traditional artist. Because even the inventors must be followers first, it is of primary importance for the understanding of an innovative artist's work and intentions to know how the artist's predominant interests were shaped by his immediate intellectual milieu. Ignorance of the facts of this milieu on the part of a critic can easily bring him to attribute too much importance to inaccurately delineated sources and, consequently, to misrepresent the artist's intentions.

As I intend to show in this book, the immediate influence of certain developments in the visual arts on the poetry of William Carlos Williams has been pervasive, and very literal in nature. Williams was throughout his life fascinated with painting, and with the visual object. The extent of their influence encompasses, due to the length of Williams' active life as a poet, such a remarkable span of years that it would be impossible to treat all the aspects with more than summary attention in a study of moderate proportions. I have therefore limited the scope of my remarks to the delineation of what were without doubt the two movements which had the earliest as well as the most durable impact on this poet: Cubism and the work of Alfred Stieglitz and the painters and theorists who had grouped themselves around him. I have moreover limited my discussion to the first twenty years of Williams' more than five decades of creative activity. I therefore virtually ignore such important secondary influences on the poet's work as the later manifestations of Dada, and Surrealism. Furthermore, since I concentrate on the poems from 1909 to 1929, I do not discuss the visual sources for such later works as *Paterson* and *Pictures from Brueghel*. I believe, however, that the initial influence of Cubism and the Stieglitz group remained so central throughout Williams' life that any discussion of the ostensible sources for these later poems will have to remain secondary to a discussion of the elements of structure and theory on which I concentrate in this book.

In order to understand why an artist was influenced more directly by certain movements than by others which were perhaps equally accessible, one must try to reconstruct the pattern of his dominant interests, the nature of his immediate cultural milieu, and the theories about certain movements which were current when the artist first underwent their influence. One must, in other words, go back into the formative years of the artist's life and experience them as much as possible through his own eyes. I have, therefore, refrained from using current scholarly views concerning the significance of Cubism or the other art movements which came to the fore during the early years of this century. Instead I have, wherever possible, used only those theoretical or interpretive remarks which may be assumed to reflect with some accuracy the things Williams himself might have read or heard about these movements when they were still new and puzzling to him. Certain statements about the aims of the Cubists, promulgated by Apollinaire and others, for instance, which scholars now consider inaccurate, misleading, or too simplistic, are deliberately perpetuated in this book, while recent scholarly reinterpretations of the meaning and aims of Cubism, are, as deliberately, ignored. For the same reason I refrain from discussing certain tempting parallels between the ideas of the writers and painters discussed in this book and some basic features of certain philosophical systems such as phenomenology, not because such comparisons are not significant, but because these theories were not among the sources to which Williams was likely to have had immediate access. The philosophy of Bergson, too, is alluded to only insofar as his ideas were used, and mostly misused, by certain painters and theorists to give their preoccupations an aura of legitimacy.

I do not intend to prove that Williams was not influenced by literary sources. Obviously his work was as profoundly shaped by the writing of his time as by its painting. This book simply hopes to illuminate some of the ways in which painting, in its own right, influenced Williams' literary concerns, and to indicate how an awareness of this fact contributes to our understanding of his poetry. I do not claim to overthrow any existing theories about his work; this book is rather supplementary to much of what has already been written about

Williams. It explains those features of his work which cannot be approached by means of the limited focus of a purely literary study. The development of painting following Cézanne created a tracery of influences which extends far beyond the visual arts proper, and which has, in one way or another, left its imprint on the structure of literature as well. The full extent of these influences will always be difficult to assess, but with few exceptions even the major patterns discernible have not yet been studied with sufficient care. I trust that the evidence presented in these pages to show the influence exerted by certain styles of painting on the development of William Carlos Williams' poetry will be sufficiently convincing to prove that the relationships between various creative media need to be studied as carefully as the patterns of influence which exist within each of the separate branches of art. As Williams once said, ultimately all we can do is to try to understand something in its natural shapes and colors. To do that we may have to go beyond the immediate context of our personal means of expression.

ACKNOWLEDGMENTS

I am especially grateful for the help, advice, and encouragement of Thomas F. Parkinson during all the stages of the preparation of this book, and for the many invaluable hints and suggestions of Roy Harvey Pearce at the time of its completion.

For information about certain details and for the necessary permissions to reprint or reproduce I would like to thank Miss Georgia O'Keeffe, Miss Doris Bry, Mrs. Roselle Davis, Mrs. Dorothy Norman, Mrs. William Carlos Williams, Miss Norma Berger, Mrs. Edith Gregor Halpert and Mr. Donald C. Gallup.

CONTENTS

LIST OF PLATES

Cubism, Stieglitz, and the Early Poetry of William Carlos Williams

I. THE NEW YORK AVANT GARDE/1910-1917

*I*T IS FREQUENTLY assumed that before the advent of the 1920's American literature was still living in the nineteenth century, and that it took World War I to shake the United States out of its cultural isolation in 1917, when thousands of young Americans were sent overseas. For many writers, for E. E. Cummings, for Dos Passos, for Hemingway, and others, this was indeed the case. But the emphasis given to the expatriates of the Twenties in such works of literary anecdote and autobiography as *Exile's Return* has obscured the fact that the formative years of several important figures in twentieth century American literature—Wallace Stevens, Marianne Moore, Sherwood Anderson, and William Carlos Williams—fell before America's entry into the war. The main reason for this unawareness is the assumption that these writers, too, were forced to find their guiding spirit in the liberating milieu of the Twenties because the earlier decades had not produced an inspiring literary atmosphere. But this view can be maintained only if we limit ourselves to a consideration of strictly literary influences.

After the war, the young American novelists and poets were kept busy trying to turn their experiences in Europe into literature, or studying the remarkable experiments of James Joyce and other European literary figures. They knew the work of Picasso, Braque, and Francis Picabia, and they eyed the Dadaists with interest. But Cubism, although still strange to many, had lost the attraction of novelty. Too much was happening, in the realm of popular culture and in literature itself, to make a young writer feel that he might have to look for other sources of

3

inspiration. In earlier years the situation had been different. Long before the beginning of the "Jazz Age," some of the older poets had found, if on a much smaller scale, a community which proved to be equally adventurous, equally unbridled in its celebration of "sex, Jazz and alcohol," and unparalleled in its revolutionary nature.[1] But they had found this climate of experimentation among the painters, not in literary circles. In the wake of the Armory Show of 1913, that exhibition which "contained so much that was fresh, new, original—eccentric, if you prefer," that it caused a surge of "heated controversy" throughout the arts,[2] the painters in New York created an atmosphere of artistic daring with which the literary world could not compete.

Certainly, the first decade of this century was a particularly bleak one for American poetry. The magazines which published verse coasted along on the work of writers who thinly echoed the already thin "acceptable" poetry of the preceding decennia. As a result, the talents of a younger generation of poets remained dormant, their work as uninteresting as that of the established writers around them. Although many poets write much of their most significant work during their twenties, these poets produced little that was not puerile—and they knew it. Wallace Stevens expressed their despondency accurately in 1909, in a letter to his future wife: "I went by myself to the National Academy. It is refreshing to pass through galleries so multi-colored; but the pictures, taken one by one, were hardly worth the trouble. . . . The artists must be growing as stupid as the poets. What would one lover of color and form and the earth and

[1] See page 33.

[2] Arthur Jerome Eddy, *Cubists and Post-Impressionism* (Chicago 1914), 1.

4

men and women do to such trash?"[3] No such person was yet to be forthcoming in literature to inspire the young poets, but even as Stevens was writing his letter, not just one, but a whole group of lovers "of color and form and the earth" were hard at work in painting to wipe out the "trash" he deplored so much. Soon Marianne Moore, Williams, Stevens, and a number of others were to turn away from the sterility of the literary atmosphere around them and to seize upon the hints of innovation in the visual arts which began to filter through to them from 1909 onward. Within a few years the revolutionary work of the painters in Paris, the work of Cézanne, the Fauves, and the Cubists swept these poets headlong into the twentieth century. Under these influences they began to sever their more obvious ties with the English romantics, realizing, as Yeats was telling them, that all the while they had been "too far from Paris," because it was "from Paris that nearly all the great influences in art and literature have come, from the time of Chaucer until now."[4]

Among the poets in this group who were to be influenced by the new forms of painting, the case of William Carlos Williams is perhaps the most striking. He was without doubt the one who attempted most literally to transpose the properties of the new forms of painting to poetry. It is indeed precisely this very literal attitude of Williams which enabled him to create a new kind of poetry, to become one of the most original poets of this century. He proved once more that the great innovators in the arts are those who can adapt the suggestions presented by the world around them to media or disciplines which seem by current standards inappropriate to their

[3] Wallace Stevens, *Letters*, ed. Holly Stevens (New York 1966), 116.

[4] Quoted in Harriet Monroe, *A Poet's Life* (New York 1938), 337.

use. They "imitate" with what seem to their contemporaries to be improper tools. Williams became one of the great literary innovators because he did just that.

Williams' interest in painting did not develop suddenly. Like Stevens he had been fascinated with the visual arts from his childhood. His mother had studied painting in Paris, and continued to paint, if infrequently, during Williams' youth. "I've always held her as a mythical figure," Williams has said, "her interest in art became my interest in art."[5] From his early youth he was visually directed. His observation of shapes and retention of visual experiences were keen. In his *Autobiography*, written when he was nearly seventy, he recalls how as a boy he saw his mother paint "an outdoor study of a twig of yellow and red crab-apples hanging from a nail,"[6] and how, in search of the anatomical secrets of women, he studied Gustave Doré's illustrations to Dante's *Divine Comedy*, although the text escaped him. Before he had "even the slightest intention of writing, or of doing anything in the arts," he tried his hand at painting. "Mother painted a little and both Ed [his brother] and I consequently painted, using her old tubes and palette which we found in the attic."[7] At the University of Pennsylvania, Williams became art editor of his classbook, contributing a number of drawings. In autobiographical remarks about his youth, reminiscences of boyhood experiences in an artist's studio, his early friendship with the painter Charles Demuth, and trips to museums both in New York and in Europe feature largely. "The painters especially have been prominent among my friends,"

[5] William Carlos Williams, *I Wanted To Write a Poem*, ed. Edith Heal (Boston 1958), 16.

[6] William Carlos Williams, *Autobiography* (New York 1951), 10.

[7] *Ibid.*, 59.

he always emphasized, "in fact I almost became a painter, as my mother had been before me, and had it not been that it was easier to transport a manuscript than a wet canvas, the balance might have been tilted the other way."[8] Even around 1913 he still "did a little painting now and then."[9] Williams was, in other words, ready to be influenced by the new styles of painting during the 1910's. The picture of these years as a grey cultural age for the majority of Americans may indeed be accurate, but for a small circle of poets and writers in or near New York during those years, the opposite was true. Williams was an enthusiastic and open-eyed, if occasionally baffled, member of this group.

Cubism, Futurism, and the indeterminate mass of styles indiscriminately classified at the time as post-impressionism were introduced to the general American public in the huge and immensely successful International Exhibition of Modern Art at the 69th Regiment Armory on Lexington Avenue in New York. The exhibition opened on February 17, 1913, and remained for three months a source of shock and amusement for thousands of Americans in New York, Chicago, and Boston. With true philistine enthusiasm, the culture-loving populace of these cities crowded to the show, to laugh at the paintings and denounce their degeneracy. The organizers were prepared for such a reaction. A general public that considered the painters of the Ashcan School outrageously experimental could not be expected to welcome Picasso or Kandinsky. But the money collected from those who came to laugh paid for the education of the few who came to see. The Armory Show was of central importance to the development of Ameri-

[8] William Carlos Williams, *Selected Essays* (New York 1954), xiv.
    [9] *Autobiography*, 139.

7

can art, and its story has been told frequently and extensively,[10] and does not need to be repeated here. Its impact on the painters is beyond dispute. But equally important is that the event disturbed the complacency of many in other fields as well. In a letter to the *New York Evening Post* a week after the Armory Show had opened, Joel E. Spingarn, then professor of philosophy at Columbia University, remarked: "I confess that when I left the exhibition my feeling was not merely one of excitement; but mingled with it was a real depression at the thought that no other artists shared this courage of the painters of our time. How timid seemed our poetry and our drama and our prose fiction; how conventional and pusillanimous our literary and dramatic criticism; how faded and academic and anemic every other form of artistic expression."[11] This attitude was of course incomprehensible to the majority of the public, including the intelligentsia. Most of the intellectual establishment disassociated itself vigorously from the show's "anarchy." But to Williams, Stevens, and the other poets and writers who were dissatisfied with the state of American letters, Spingarn's reaction was understandable. They had recently found a rickety platform for dissent in *Poetry*, but their rebelliousness was based not so much on new ideas as on a vague awareness of the bankruptcy of established forms of writing. They knew that it was time to do something new, but what they should be doing they did not know. Moreover, *Poetry* itself was hardly adventurous. Even as early as 1913 William Carlos

[10] See for instance Milton W. Brown, *The Story of the Armory Show* (Greenwich, Conn., 1963), the *Catalogue of the 50th Anniversary Exhibition of the Armory Show* (Utica and New York 1963), and the special section on the Armory Show in *Art in America*, LI, 1 (February 1963), 29-63.

[11] Quoted in Brown, *The Story of the Armory Show*, 156.

Williams was writing to Harriet Monroe to say: "I am startled to see that you are fast gravitating towards the usual editorial position."[12] For really new and imaginative discoveries one had to go to the painters.

"There was at that time a great surge of interest in the arts generally before the First World War," Williams recalled later, "New York was seething with it. Painting took the lead. It came to a head for us in the famous 'Armory Show' of 1913."[13] To Williams, half a century after the event, the show was still a vivid memory: "It is fifty years since the famous Armory Show shocked New Yorkers into a realization, a visualization, that their world had been asleep while the art world had undergone a revolution. In Paris, painters from Cézanne to Pisarro had been painting their revolutionary canvases for fifty or more years but it was not until I clapped my eyes on Marcel Duchamp's *Nude Descending a Staircase* that I burst out laughing from the relief it brought me! I felt as if an enormous weight had been lifted from my spirit for which I was infinitely grateful."[14]

Had the Armory Show been an isolated manifestation of the new developments in painting, its challenge to the other arts might soon have been forgotten. But modern art had first found its way to New York several years earlier, and the show was merely its first large-scale surfacing. For those who seriously wanted to study the new forms of expression in the visual arts, there were to be many more opportunities, mostly due to the efforts of the famous photographer Alfred Stieglitz. It would not be unfair to say that Stieglitz was largely responsible for the revolutionary character of the Armory Show. He was

[12] Williams, *Selected Letters*, 22.
[13] Williams, *Autobiography*, 134.
[14] Williams, "Recollections," *Art in America*, LI, 1 (February 1963), 52.

not one of the official organizers of the exhibition, but for a number of years prior to 1913 he had used the gallery, of which he was the director, to make the more inquisitive elements within the artistic community of New York familiar with the work of the Fauves and the Cubists. Among the artists who had frequented his gallery during those years were several of the organizers of the Armory Show, including Arthur B. Davies, its "guiding genius."

Stieglitz was content to remain in the background during the wave of publicity surrounding the exhibition, but he was well aware of the role he had played in making it a reality. Writing to one of his acquaintances about the show he emphasized that it was "really the outcome of the work going on at '291' for many years," and added: "One thing is sure, the people at large and for that matter also the artists, etc. have been made to realize the importance of the work that has been going on at '291' and in *Camera Work*. This much the Exhibition accomplished for us."[15]

The Little Galleries of the Photo-Secession, more conveniently called "291" after their address on Fifth Avenue, had originally been opened in 1905 by Stieglitz to show photography as art. But "tired of the 'swelled heads' the photographers had gotten," he decided late in 1907 to exhibit drawings by Pamela Coleman Smith, and, as he said, "destroy the idea that the Photo-Secession as well as myself were dedicated solely to the exhibition of photo-

[15] Unpublished letter, quoted in Robert Doty, *Photo-Secession: Photography as a Fine Art* (Rochester 1960), 63. For a fuller account of Stieglitz's role in the organization of the Armory Show see Beaumont Newhall, "Stieglitz and 291," *Art in America*, LI, 1 (February 1963), 48-51.

graphs."[16] Eduard Steichen, who was in Paris at that time, and who had been among the original members of Photo-Secession, offered to send a selection of drawings by Rodin. Stieglitz accepted immediately, and with their exhibition in January 1908 the development of 291 as a center for avant garde activity in all the arts began. Stieglitz was already known as the most daring experimenter in photography, and in the magazine he edited, *Camera Work*, he had recorded the development of photography in detail. Now he became the mentor of the experimental artists in New York, no matter in what medium they chose to express themselves. He showed the work of Matisse in April 1908 and February 1910, lithographs by Toulouse-Lautrec in December 1909, paintings and drawings by Henri Rousseau in November 1910, Cézanne watercolors in March, and Picasso watercolors and drawings in April 1911. For all these artists this was their first comprehensive public showing in the United States. It is easy to imagine what kind of impression they made on young artists and writers searching for a way in which to express the incoherent sense of difference they felt between them and all that had gone before.[17]

For anyone who wanted to try something new in art, New York at the beginning of this century had not been an encouraging environment. The attitude of Sir Purdon Clarke, the director of the Metropolitan Museum of Art, who let it be known that he thought that a work by William Blake was "not worth the paper it's on," is representative of the atmosphere prevalent among the "cul-

[16] "From the Writings and Conversations of Alfred Stieglitz," compiled by Dorothy Norman, *Twice a Year*, 1 (Fall-Winter 1938), 77-110.

[17] Among those who very early found their way to Stieglitz's gallery were Alfred Kreymborg, Walter Conrad Arensberg, Djuna Barnes, Charles Demuth, and most of the painters who were later to be known as the "Stieglitz Group."

11

tural élite." "There is a state of unrest in the world," said Clarke, "in art as in all other things. It is the same in literature as in music, in painting and in sculpture. And I dislike unrest."[18]

If you did like "unrest," 291 was the place to go. In addition to the European painters, Stieglitz carefully selected from among the young Americans those who he thought were most promising, those in whom he felt he could see the makings of a real American talent. His choice was uncannily accurate. Before the year 1912 came to a close he had shown the work of Alfred Maurer, John Marin, Marsden Hartley, Arthur Dove, Max Weber, and Abraham Walkowitz.

In *Pearson's Magazine*, a few years later, Guido Bruno recalled: "In those days our eyes were baffled by the different conception of things on canvas and drawing boards. The critics of our papers, the very same ones who write at present learned treaties about Cézanne and Picasso, or Picabia and Matisse, then had only a laughing sneer for the new modern art. They made it hot for Stieglitz. They ridiculed him, abused him. . . . But Stieglitz said: 'We have to learn how to see. We all have to learn to use our eyes, and "291" is here for no other purpose than to give everybody a chance to see.' " And, Bruno continued, "I dare say that there is hardly an artist, writer, or poet in this country today who did not hasten to 291, enthusiastically and curiously whenever he came to New York."[19]

One of the most daring, and most telling, of Stieglitz's early ventures was his sponsorship of Gertrude Stein.

[18] Interview with Sir Purdon Clarke in the *New York Post* (December 30, 1908); reprinted in *Camera Work*, 26 (April 1909), 25.

[19] Guido Bruno, "The Passing of '291,' " *Pearson's Magazine*, xxxviii, 9 (March 1918), 402-03.

Stieglitz had come to know her in 1909 on a summer trip to Paris, where he had gone to survey the new developments in painting at first hand. He spent many evenings at 27 Rue de Fleurus and a few years later, in 1912, he brought out a special issue of *Camera Work* devoted entirely to two "essays" by Gertrude Stein, one on Matisse and one on Picasso. To supplement these short pieces Stieglitz included fourteen full-page reproductions of "representative paintings and sculptures" by the artists subjected to Gertrude Stein's unusual scrutiny. *Three Lives* had been published earlier (in 1910), but it was virtually unknown. The pieces in *Camera Work* constituted Gertrude Stein's first magazine publication, and rarely has an unknown, experimental author received an equally distinguished treatment. *Camera Work* was a magazine printed with scrupulous care on heavy, high-quality paper, and the reproductions it featured of photography and other art were tipped in by hand and frequently hard to distinguish from original prints. No one can accuse Stieglitz of having had any motive of financial gain in publishing that special issue. Gertrude Stein's style was not designed to encourage the casual reader. Her words tended to fall in recurrent circular, or angular, sound patterns on the page. Those who read what she wrote about Matisse got caught in a whirlpool of chubby syllables and hard words, and all they seemed to get for their trouble was the knowledge that Matisse was someone "greatly expressing something struggling," and Picasso "one whom some were certainly following." In an editorial Stieglitz emphasized that the articles themselves, "and not either the subjects with which they deal or the illustrations that accompany them, are the *raison d'être* of this special issue." The "intellectual and esthetic attitude" of which the articles are a part, he said,

13

"found its first expression in the field of painting." Gertrude Stein, whose art is literature, and "whose raw material is words," offers us "a decipherable clew to that intellectual and esthetic attitude which underlies and inspires the movement upon one phase of which they are comments and of the extending development of which they are themselves an integral part."

Although *Camera Work* was in terms of its circulation a "little magazine," it was well known among artists, writers, and even the general public, as the hilarious responses to Gertrude Stein's work in the press showed. Her work was used from then on as an example of literary Cubism. During the time of the Armory Show her "portrait" of Mabel Dodge gained a fairly wide circulation and that, together with the special issue of *Camera Work*, gave her all the publicity she needed to be mentioned repeatedly alongside the painters of the Armory Show, mostly in spoofs. The *Chicago Tribune* of February 8, 1913, published this quatrain:

> I called the canvas *Cow with Cud*
> And hung it on the line,
> Altho' to me 'twas vague as mud
> 'Twas clear to Gertrude Stein.[20]

At the "First Annual Vanishing Day" of the "Academy of Misapplied Arts" on March 22, 1913, a party which brought most of the leading members of the National Academy of Design together in a ritual designed to bury the new art before it could do further harm, one artist presented a work called "Cubist painting, cubist painting, cubist painting."[21] In *The Cubies' ABC*, another Armory

[20] Quoted in Brown, *The Story of the Armory Show*, 111.
[21] *Ibid.*, 115.

Show parody, Gertrude Stein is included among the painters as the only "Futurist scribe."[22]

After the Armory Show, 291 and *Camera Work*, the magazine which represented it, remained the most important sources for information about the new art. On March 3, 1913 Stieglitz wrote to Marsden Hartley: "I simply cannot get a moment for myself. You have no idea what is going on in New York. '291' is still the storm center in spite of the Big Show."[23] The small rooms on Fifth Avenue were almost always filled with people arguing about aspects of the new art. Painters like Hartley, John Marin, or Charles Demuth would be there, and always one could find Stieglitz among them.

In the years between the Armory Show and America's entry into the war, 291 continued to expand. With unflagging enthusiasm it spread the theories of the new art among the avant garde. *Camera Work* was undoubtedly one of the most important forces in American cultural life at that time. In 1909 it had begun to publish articles which discussed and explained the theories behind the work of Matisse and Cézanne. The aims of Fauvism, Cubism, and Futurism soon became recurrent topics of discussion. Quotations from and references to the writings of Bergson, Kandinsky, Gleizes, and Apollinaire became common fare. In the March 1910 issue two of Matisse's drawings were reproduced and were followed by works of Cézanne, Picasso, Walkowitz, De Zayas (Plate 1), and others. Sometimes there were brilliant color reproductions of, for example, watercolors by John Marin, or drawings by Rodin—the latter so sensitive in

[22] See John Malcolm Brinnin, *The Third Rose* (New York, Evergreen ed. 1961), 184.

[23] Unpublished letter, Stieglitz Archive, Collection of American Literature, Yale University Library.

their approximation of the actual tints as to make it difficult not to confuse them with originals.

The special issue of 1913, published in the wake of the Armory Show, can serve as example of the scope of *Camera Work*. The issue opens with Gertrude Stein's "Portrait of Mabel Dodge at the Villa Curonia," a piece in a style as unusual as her portraits of Picasso and Matisse. This is followed by an article by Mabel Dodge, "Speculations," in which she emphasizes again that "Gertrude Stein is doing with words what Picasso is doing with paint. She is impelling language to induce new states of consciousness and in doing so language becomes with her a creative art rather than a mirror of history." To present her impressions "she chooses words for their inherent quality rather than for their accepted meaning." What she does is "a working proof of the Bergson theory of intuition. She does not go after words—she waits—and lets them come to her, and they do."

In the article that follows, "Modern Art and the Public," Gabrielle Buffet, the wife of the painter Francis Picabia, discusses the difficulties besetting the artist in his attempts to make the public see the positive qualities in his paintings, and the necessity of forcing the public to forego its desire "to find some objective point of contact between the title of a picture and the picture itself."

Maurice Aisen, in "The Latest Evolution in Art and Picabia," warns that "the dominant note of the present epoch is revolutionary not only in the plastic arts and in music, but in everything that exists." In "The Renaissance of the Irrational," Benjamin de Casseres, always one of the most unbridled of those writing for *Camera Work*, chants that the philosophy of the new era must be that "the absolute is change." "The intellect is bankrupt," he feels, "life itself explains life." He adds: "Each moment is a near-at-hand divine event in which the whole creation is incarnated." For him "the real fathers of the cubists and futurists" are Emerson, Thoreau, and Whitman.

The painter and architect Oscar Bluemner, finally, in the article that follows, "Audiator et Altera Pars: Some Plain Sense on the Modern Art Movement," speculates about the long-range influence of the Armory Show. The show made many people realize, he says, that "it is the vision of things and of their relation to one another and that of ourselves to them, in which modern life and art differs from the past." Artists will have to take into account the discoveries of science, "to see and to feel the world, as science reveals it today. In this way originates the new vision of external objects and of imagination. There is a necessary analogy between the impressions of the artist and the scientific and philosophical evolution going on."

To complement the articles in this special issue of *Camera Work* there are nine full-page reproductions of paintings: three by Cézanne, one by Van Gogh, three by Picasso (including his portrait of Gertrude Stein), and one by Picabia.

Stieglitz himself and the people most closely associated with him were in close touch with developments in the major European art centers. As early as 1913 Stieglitz was corresponding with Kandinsky, trying among other things to arrange for a show of his work at 291. His correspondence with Marsden Hartley, who was in Europe between 1912 and 1914, and who became closely linked with the German Expressionists during that period, indicates that he was well acquainted with the volume *Der Blaue Reiter*, published in 1912 by Kandinsky and Franz Marc, as well as with Kandinsky's essay *Über das Geistige in der Kunst*. Correspondence between Marius de Zayas and Stieglitz, moreover, shows that Stieglitz was familiar at a very early date with the writings of such people as Apollinaire, and was in fact reading *Les Soirées de Paris* regularly. De Zayas, who was in Paris for long periods of time between 1910 and 1914, was doing extremely important scouting for Stieglitz, sizing up the experiments, reporting, arranging for exhibitions to be sent to 291, hunting up new tendencies in art. In one of his letters he said: "I am working hard in making these people understand the convenience of a commerce of ideas with America. And I want to absorb the spirit of what they are doing to bring it to '291.' We need a closer contact with Paris, there is no question about it. The 'Soirées de Paris' is going to publish four of my caricatures in the next number: Vollard's, Apollinaire's, Picabia's and yours. They asked for them and I thought it would be good for all of us to really get in with this crowd."[24]

Alfred Kreymborg was one of the young men with literary ambitions who had very early been drawn to Stieglitz and 291. In *Troubadour* he recalls how in 1910[25] Marsden Hartley brought him to the dining room of the Prince George Hotel to be introduced to Stieglitz, during one of the photographer's famous lunchtime séances: "There they were, carelessly grouped about the table: Not only Marsden and Krimmie [Kreymborg himself], but several other painters who, along with the man from Maine, were destined to play leading roles in the revolution of American art: Max Weber, John Marin, Arthur Dove, A. Walkowitz and Eduard Steichen (Carl Sandburg's brother-in-law). Several other *habitués* were pres-

[24] Unpublished letter, July 9, 1914, Stieglitz Archive, Yale.

[25] Kreymborg never gives specific dates, but he recalls how on his first entrance into 291 the room was hung with drawings by Rodin. The second Rodin exhibition took place in April 1910.

ent: Charles Caffin, the gentlemanly art critic, Marius de Zayas, the uncanny Mexican caricaturist, Paul Strand, the moody photographer, and Paul Haviland, a dreamer in ceramics. If any man was absent he was sure to be there some other time."[26]

Kreymborg from that time on became a frequent caller at 291. "It was the address on Fifth Avenue to which one often referred in answer to the demand: Where are you going? And one added cordially: Come along and see the Cézannes, Matisses, Brancusis, Picassos, Picabias. Or the Marins, Webers, Walkowitzes, Hartleys, O'Keeffes. As there were no exhibitions of his photographs, one didn't say the Stieglitzes. But one did say Stieglitz. These two syllables described and represented the perennial inspiration of the haunt."[27] Kreymborg here met "additional artists who were to influence him later on: Charles Demuth, the Zorachs, Samuel Halpert, Man Ray, McDonald Wright." Kreymborg had been floundering disastrously among the poets of the literary establishment. When he had shown his first attempts at free verse to Joyce Kilmer, this honored member of the Poetry Society of America had rebuked him by saying that if "metre and rhyme had been good enough for the masters," they should certainly be satisfactory to a budding poet. Now, at 291, Kreymborg found himself in an atmosphere where no one bothered much with "the masters" but a great deal with what was new and fresh: "To Krimmie, among others, the gallery appealed as the one place in town for the study of the birth, development and tendencies of modern art. He gradually learned that the lines of painting and sculpture complemented the lines

[26] Alfred Kreymborg, *Troubadour* (Sagamore Press, New York 1957; originally published in 1925), 126.
[27] *Ibid.*, 127.

19

of music and poetry; that, without drawing needless parallels, one could readily trace a relationship proving that many artists of the age, no matter what their medium, were seeking similar fundamentals and evolving individual forms. One did not have to be a painter to be at home in the gallery."[28] Kreymborg's experience at 291 closely paralleled and in some ways anticipated William Carlos Williams' introduction to the new art. The two poets were soon to meet.

During the summer of 1913 Man Ray and Samuel Halpert went out to the Palisades in New Jersey and rented a shack at Grantwood, among "picturesque little houses with fruit trees in between,"[29] within the boundaries of Ridgefield. Kreymborg joined them there, and soon there were plans for a "magazine of the arts." An acquaintance of Man Ray knew where an old printing press was to be found, and arrangements were made to ship it out to Grantwood. Kreymborg began looking for material, writing among others to John Cournos, who had settled in London. Cournos promised to talk with Ezra Pound, and not long before the printing press was scheduled to arrive Kreymborg received a package from Pound containing the materials for a small anthology of poems. Pound insisted that it should be published under the title *Des Imagistes*. In the accompanying letter he told Kreymborg to look up William Carlos Williams, "my one remaining pal in America—get in touch with old Bull—he lives in a hole called Rutherford, New Jersey."[30]

When the printing press arrived, Williams was among those who welcomed it.[31] Unfortunately the old press had

[28] *Ibid.*, 127-28.
[29] Man Ray, *Self Portrait* (Boston 1963), 30.
[30] Kreymborg, *Troubadour*, 157.
[31] See Man Ray, *Self Portrait*, 40.

been ruined in transport and the idea for a handprinted magazine had to be abandoned. But the press had served a useful purpose: it had brought together some of the people who were to transform Grantwood into a second meeting place of the avant garde. Kreymborg meanwhile managed to interest Albert and Charles Boni in his plans for a magazine and *The Glebe* appeared, publishing among other things a one-act comedy by Charles Demuth and, in February 1914, *Des Imagistes*.

At meetings of contributors to *Rogue*, the little magazine edited by Allan and Louise Norton, Kreymborg met such people as Wallace Stevens, Mina Loy, and Walter Conrad Arensberg. With Arensberg, Kreymborg began to make plans for still another magazine, to be called *Others*. By this time the new styles of painting had begun to interest an ever larger number of artists. The activities of 291 were beginning to spill over into other places: Charles Daniel, a retired "saloon keeper" with a passionate fondness for art, spurred on by such people as Alanson Hartpence, decided to open a gallery. "Two Ninety One was the original impulse of my going into the modern world of art," Daniel wrote: "Aside from the pictures, the attitude of Mr. Stieglitz toward art and life made a deep impression upon me."[32] Daniel began to show the work of Demuth, Man Ray, Walkowitz, and others of the Americans in the Stieglitz group. The Modern Gallery, which was to be run by Marius de Zayas, announced that it would be open "for the sale of paintings of the most advanced character of the modern art movement—negro sculptures—pre-conquest Mexican art —photography," and stressed that "the *Modern Gallery* is but an additional expression of '291.' "[33]

[32] *Camera Work*, 47 (January 1915).
[33] 291, 1 (March 1915).

21

The avant garde movement began to develop three centers: The first remained as always 291, with activity centering on Stieglitz and his American painters, as well as de Zayas and Francis Picabia; a second became the group around Walter Conrad Arensberg, including Mina Loy and the painters Marcel Duchamp and Albert Gleizes, as well as Wallace Stevens, when he was in town; the third developed in Grantwood, which had become a full-fledged artist's colony, and where Kreymborg began to publish *Others*, with the help of William Carlos Williams, who was making frequent trips out to the shacks in the Palisades. The painters and poets who belonged to these three very loose, and at that time by no means recognized groupings, moved very freely among the groups. 291 Fifth Avenue, Arensberg's apartment on West 67th Street, and Grantwood, New Jersey, can therefore best be seen as three different locales for the activities of a larger group, most of whose members knew each other.

Arensberg's apartment had already become famous for the amazing collection of Cubist paintings on its walls. Arensberg furthermore took it upon himself to introduce his artist friends to each other when the opportunity arose. Wallace Stevens, who had been a classmate of Arensberg at Harvard, wrote the following to his wife about such an occasion: "Walter Arensberg telephoned yesterday afternoon and asked me to take dinner with him at the Brevoort with Marcel Duchamp, the man who painted *The Nude Descending A Stair-Case*. Duchamp is using the Arensbergs' apartment as a studio during the summer. . . . After dinner, we went up to the Arensbergs' apartment and looked at some of Duchamp's things. I made very little out of them. But naturally, without sophistication in that direction, and with only a very rudimentary feeling about art, I expect little of myself.

Duchamp speaks very little English. When the three of us spoke French, it sounded like sparrows around a pool of water. . . ."[34]

Arensberg had given Kreymborg the impetus to start publishing *Others*. They had decided upon a magazine that would give a chance to those writers who, due to their interest in new forms of expression, were being ignored by most of the established magazines, and even, to a large extent, by *Poetry*. Stevens, Arensberg himself, Kreymborg, Williams, Mina Loy, Alanson Hartpence, Maxwell Bodenheim, and Marianne Moore were some of the poets appearing in the early issues of *Others*, as well as, somewhat incongruously, T.S. Eliot, whose manuscript of *Portrait of a Lady* had one day fallen unexpectedly out of an envelope with a letter from Pound. Arensberg decided at the last moment not to become involved in the editorial aspects of *Others*, but he offered to take care of the printing costs for at least the first year.

Although *Others* did not quarrel openly with the ideas associated with Imagism, it largely ignored them in favor of techniques developed from artistic sources within the New York avant garde. Imagism, which had recently been abandoned by its principal champion, Ezra Pound, and which had fluttered spasmodically in the pages of *Poetry*, had at first been mostly an English venture. By far the largest number of poems included in *Des Imagistes*, including those of Pound and H.D., had been written in England. In America, Imagism had undoubtedly given an early impetus to a number of poets, including Williams, but with the introduction of modern art to New York, and the exciting years that followed, the concepts of Imagism, which, for that matter had itself been largely

[34] *Letters*, 185.

23

inspired by what was happening in the visual arts, became more or less self-evident for the poets in the Metropolitan area. The tenets of Imagism, as listed in *Poetry* in two separate articles by F. S. Flint and Ezra Pound,[35] were all contained in the theories associated with the movements of painting that took their cue from Cézanne. Flint, in this instance, seems to have functioned primarily as a mouthpiece for Pound's ideas. He could emphasize as much as he wished that "the *imagistes* admitted that they were contemporaries of the Post-Impressionists and the Futurists, but [that] they had nothing in common with these schools"; the facts are quite different.

The first of Flint's requirements for an Imagist, the "direct treatment of the 'Thing,' whether subjective or objective," was a basic concern of Cézanne's, and of nearly all the painters who came after him. They considered it the artist's primary function to analyze an object, a locale, or even an idea, without recourse to external concepts or reference to matters that do not contribute to a direct understanding of the "thing" which is being treated. Even in America, in *Camera Work*, this goal was being stressed as early as 1909. Hutchins Hapgood in the *New York Globe* pointed out that in the work of such painters as Max Weber, who was himself a follower of the Parisian movements, "there is an attempt to render plastic the inner constitution of objects. . . . Instead of concentrating on the atmosphere," Hapgood said, "there is a concentration on the form."[36]

Flint's second Imagist rule, "to use absolutely no word that does not contribute to the presentation," can hardly be considered different in intention from the "process of

[35] *Poetry*, I, 6 (March 1913), 198-206.
[36] Hutchins Hapgood, "Hospitality in Art," reprinted in *Camera Work*, 38 (April 1912), 43.

simplification" which Charles H. Caffin in the January 1909 issue of *Camera Work* considers one of the main features of Matisse's work. In fact Caffin attributes to Matisse the same derivation from Oriental sources which is usually included in discussions of Imagism.

As for the freedom from established versification and rhythmic patterns which is considered a major liberating feature of the Imagist creed: one can hardly assume that someone aware of the freedoms which the painters had been taking with the established rules of "pictorial" art would not have come to the idea that the "laws" of poetry could be treated with a similar impunity.

In any case, the derivation of Imagism need not be resolved here. (One could point to its sources in late nineteenth century French poetry, but since poetry and painting in France were already becoming intricately related during the last half of that century, this would only emphasize the danger of easy generalization.) It would seem clear that the intensity of avant garde activity and theorizing in New York beginning with the Armory Show left Imagism a rather unexciting and even redundant bone to chew on for poets like Williams, who as much as anyone else was aware of the truth of Mabel Dodge's statement in *Camera Work* that "nearly every thinking person nowadays is in revolt against something, because the craving of the individual is for further consciousness, and because consciousness is expanding and is bursting through the molds that have held it up to now."[37]

The first issue of *Others* was welcomed by most critics with a hearty laugh. These critics, according to Kreymborg, "even accepted Imagism, now under the expert guidance of Amy Lowell, in preference to these *Others.*

[37] *Camera Work*, Special Number (June 1913), 7.

. . . Even some of the Imagists were outraged."[38] Amy Lowell contributed, but let it be known that she did not approve of most of the other contributors. Williams' feeling was that when Imagism became, as Pound remarked, "Amygism," it lost its vitality; moreover, too much was happening to bother with rules.

At Grantwood, Williams and Kreymborg had become very close friends. Williams recalls: "Several writers were involved, but the focus of my own enthusiasm was the house occupied by Alfred and Gertrude Kreymborg to which, on every possible occasion, I went madly in my flivver to help with the magazine which had saved my life as a writer."[39] Elsewhere Williams remarks that at that time everything he wrote was done with *Others* in mind.

Among the people Williams could expect to find at Grantwood from time to time were Man Ray, Arensberg, Duchamp, Mina Loy, and Marianne Moore. "I'd sneak away mostly on Sundays to join the gang, show what I had written and sometimes help Kreymborg with the make-up," Williams recalls. "We'd have arguments over cubism which would fill an afternoon. There was a comparable whipping up of interest in the structure of the poem. It seemed daring to omit capitals at the head of each poetic line. Rhyme went by the board."[40] At the same time 291 was not forgotten. Writing to Stieglitz from Grantwood on July 16, 1915, Kreymborg regretted that his more or less rural existence prevented him from visiting 291 as often as he wished to. But,

[38] Kreymborg, *Troubadour*, 184.
[39] Williams, *Autobiography*, 135. "Gertrude" Kreymborg's name was actually Christine. Kreymborg had first met her at the home of Mr. and Mrs. Charles H. Caffin, whose protégé she was. Caffin, of course, was one of Stieglitz's most perceptive associates.
[40] *Ibid.*, 136.

Kreymborg wrote, "291 is ever a potent influence out here." Along with this letter he sent Stieglitz the first issue of *Others*, and a poem, "Cézanne," which he hoped could be used in the magazine *291*, which Stieglitz was publishing at that time.[41]

At 291, exhibitions of modern art continued as before. Indeed, to the popular comic magazine *Puck* it seemed to be *the* gathering place of snobs. One of the points *Puck* told its readers to keep in mind, in an instructive article on "How to Become a Highbrow," was always to "profess admiration for Alfred Stieglitz's Little Galleries and other artistic fakes."[42] But to Horace Traubel 291 was "the most potent expression of Art in New York"[43] and, according to Huntley Carter in *The Egoist*, the magazines published at 291 were calling attention to "the excellence of the work promoted throughout by Mr. Stieglitz, and the war-time phase of extremism."[44]

Neither praise nor derision could impede the work of the Stieglitz group. In 1913 Marius de Zayas and Paul B. Haviland published under Stieglitz's auspices an intelligent pamphlet on the nature of modern art, *A Study of the Modern Evolution of Plastic Expression*, in which they quoted such recent works as Gleizes' and Metzinger's *Du Cubisme*. In the same year J. Nilsen Laurvik published a booklet called *Is It Art?* which had the dubious distinction of being cribbed almost verbatim from articles written by Charles Caffin and Marius de Zayas for *Camera Work*. In his enthusiasm for copying the work of others, however, Laurvik made himself useful by quoting, nearly in its entirety, the *Futurist Mani-*

[41] Unpublished letter, Stieglitz Archive, Yale.

[42] *Puck* (January 8, 1916).

[43] Horace Traubel, "Stieglitz," *Conservator*, xxvii, 10 (December 1916), 137.

[44] Huntley Carter, "Two Ninety One," *The Egoist*, iii, 3 (March 1916).

festo which had been published on April 11, 1910 over the signatures of Boccioni, Carrà, Russolo, Balla, and Severini.

Camera Work continued to print pages from Bergson's *Creative Evolution* and from his essay on laughter, as well as an excerpt from Kandinsky's *The Spiritual in Art*, in addition to a large number of essays on painters and painting. It published more works by Gertrude Stein and "Aphorisms on Futurism" by Mina Loy. It also continued its helpful, but in retrospect often rather cruel, habit of reprinting everything that was being said in the daily press about the exhibitions at 291. The misjudgments of most critics were colossal. But with the issue of January 1915 regular publication came to an end. There were to be two more issues, one in 1916 and one in 1917, but as a periodical *Camera Work* virtually ceased to exist. The issues published, however, remained current among those who frequented 291, and even in 1917 we still find correspondence between Stieglitz and Marianne Moore about back issues and a subscription.

But if *Camera Work* was dying, a far more radical publishing venture sponsored by Stieglitz was about to startle New York's avant garde. Marius de Zayas had spent his time in Europe well. On his return to the United States early in 1915, he and Agnes Ernst Meyer started a magazine under Stieglitz's sponsorship, which, patterned after what de Zayas had seen in Paris, carried the experiments on which it was based far beyond their original scope. This was the magazine to which Kreymborg hoped to contribute his poem on Cézanne: 291, named after the address from which it was published. The first issue appeared in March 1915. Beautifully printed in two colors on large leaves of sturdy paper, it presented on its six pages a remarkable variety of material. The cover was a geometrical, humorously "cubist" caricature of Stieglitz by de Zayas. Inside were a drawing by Picasso; one of Apollinaire's most intricate *idéogrammes*, "Voyage," which had originally been published in *Les Soirées de Paris*; some Freudian dream sequences by Stieglitz; and several short essays, including one on "Simultanism" in art and literature, with an example of how a "polyphony of simultaneous voices" can be achieved in literature by carefully transposing the practices of Picasso and Braque to the realm of language. In its next issue 291 followed through on this concept by publishing a page on which thought flashes, in what amounts to a stream of consciousness technique, were interspersed with advertising slogans and disjointed comments of what would seem to be passers-by. Written by Katherine N. Rhoades, the piece was called "Mental Reactions." De Zayas had interconnected the words, or broken them up, by means of drawings and line structures of angular shapes; some words seemed to be falling off the page, and whole lines of type stood at odd angles to each other: the result was *les mots en liberté* with a vengeance. Typographical experiments were to continue through the twelve issues of the magazine. The illustrations consisted of cubist or nearly abstract drawings by such artists as Walkowitz, Marin, Picasso, and Braque. A sketch by Francis Picabia, an artist who was to play an ever-larger role in the direction of the magazine as well as in the avant garde circles in New York, appeared in the second issue.

Picabia had first visited New York in 1913 when he and his wife, Gabrielle Buffet, decided to take a personal look at the exhibition to which he and so many of his Parisian friends had contributed. In New York he immediately became for press and public alike the personification of what Americans considered the unruly French anarchic spirit guilty of the outlandish paintings at the

Armory Show. A celebrity, relishing the tumult he was causing, immensely excited by the violent activity of New York, and fascinated by such intricate structures as the 59th Street Bridge, Picabia, who had planned a three-week visit, stayed for nearly six months. Soon after his arrival he met Stieglitz. Gabrielle Buffet recalls: "Picabia n'en fut pas moins enchanté de rencontrer chez Alfred Stieglitz, et dans son groupe du '291 5e ave.' . . . des hommes intelligents, doués et parfaitement au courant de la vie intellectuelle d'Europe, qui l'accueillirent avec toute l'admiration, le respect et la gentillesse qu'il pouvait désirer."[45] Stieglitz immediately suggested that 291 present an exhibition of Picabia's work. Picabia, who had brought none of his paintings with him, except for the ones being shown at the Armory Show, enthusiastically went to work to record his impressions of New York in both paintings and drawings. The exhibition took place in March 1913, soon after the Armory Show.

Picabia's unrestrained search for the unusual and his strong sense of the absurdities of life found a fertile environment among the members of the Stieglitz group. Not only did he find them "parfaitement au courant de la vie intellectuelle d'Europe," they also discoursed of "thèmes fort anarchiques pour l'heure."[46] Some of the more extreme members, indeed, had as strong an affinity as Picabia to what was later to be regarded as the "Dada" spirit. Benjamin de Casseres, for instance, as early as 1912, had written in *Camera Work* that "all seriousness is a defect of vision. . . . There is no form of seriousness, even in art, that has not in it the germ of disaster for

[45] Gabrielle Buffet-Picabia, *Aires Abstraites* (Geneva 1957), 31.
[46] *Ibid.*, 168.

the mind that is a slave to it."[47] And while Picabia was in New York in 1913 de Casseres wrote: "Sanity and simplicity are the prime curses of civilization." We should, he argued, "make a religion of the artificial, the insincere, the pose. We should mock existence at each moment, mock ourselves, mock others, mock everything by the perpetual creation of fantastic and grotesque attitudes. . . ."[48]

In the special issue of *Camera Work* of 1913 which was full of serious essays on modern art, Picabia showed how much his own notions agreed with those of de Casseres. He contributed an article with the title "vers l'Amorphisme," which was a purposely pompous "essay" arguing that the implications of the attitudes underlying modern art should be explored fully and fearlessly. Form, which was the basis of Cubism, must be abolished: "La forme, voilà l'ennemi! . . . La lumière nous suffit." As an example of the new art form he "reproduced" two paintings by "Popaul Picador," in which one can see "toujours du rien, toujours blanc. . . ." The paintings were empty squares with the signature of the "artist" printed in.

In April 1915, Picabia returned again to New York. Of Cuban parentage, he managed to escape from his wartime responsibilities as chauffeur for a French general, and was ordered to Cuba, ostensibly on a mission to procure molasses for the French army. But when he arrived in New York, where he was to change ships for Havana, he found his old friends Marcel Duchamp and Albert Gleizes already there. They had managed to

[47] Benjamin de Casseres, "The Ironical in Art," *Camera Work*, 38 (April 1912), 17-19.

[48] *Camera Work*, 42-43 (April-July 1913; published Nov. 1913), 17.

escape conscription through self-imposed exile. The molasses never found its way to France; Picabia, who had forgotten all about his mission, plunged vigorously into the unrestrained life of the small avant garde artistic community of New York, joining with special enthusiasm in the experiment of 291. He began to contribute drawings which were a logical extension of the machine-like forms he had been painting since his first trip to New York. In fact, the double number of July-August 1915 is devoted entirely to these drawings. (See Plate II.) They are meticulously accurate representations of machine parts, with what Picabia considered to be appropriate titles. Thus the "Portrait d'une Jeune Fille Américaine dans l'Etat de Nudité" turns out to be a graphic representation of a spark-plug.

291 now began to print contributions from Max Jacob and Ribemont Dessaignes; texts were printed in both English and French, an indication of the international nature of the magazine and of the sophistication of its audience in New York. In fact, in August 1915 de Zayas told Stieglitz that he had sent sixty copies of the two most recent issues of 291 to Paris, "to people who have a real interest in modern art."[49] Undoubtedly more and more copies of the subsequent issues found their way to Europe. Stieglitz himself, in November 1915, at the urging of Alfred Kreymborg, sent Ezra Pound a set of 291 and some copies of *Camera Work.*

It is clear that 291 had a wide currency among the artists in New York. Its proto-Dada nature was well suited to the festively anarchic spirit there. In many ways New York City at this time closely resembled Zurich, that other gathering place for fugitives from the war. Gabrielle Buffet gives a vivid account of the art world of New York as she and her husband found it on

[49] Unpublished letter, August 16, 1915, Stieglitz Archive, Yale.

their arrival in 1915: "Nous fûmes dès notre arrivée incorporés dans une bande hétéroclite et internationale où se côtoyaient des objecteurs de conscience de toute condition et de toute nationalité, dans un déchaînement inimaginable de sexualité, de jazz et d'alcool. . . . Il subsistait pourtant dans cette foire internationale un îlot de grâce où la vie des arts et de l'esprit se trouva préservée et stimulée, et connut même, en marge des milieux et des manifestations officiels, une activité exceptionelle autant que révolutionnaire. Un petit nombre d'artistes, venus d'Europe pour la plupart, dont Duchamp et Picabia étaient les vedettes incontestées, se groupaient autour d'Alfred Stieglitz dans sa Galerie 291, Fifth Avenue, et aussi chez W.C. et Lou Arensberg."[50] In these circles, Gabrielle Buffet emphasizes, "on . . . accueillait avec une curiosité sympathique souvent quelque peu inquiète les propositions les plus outrancières et des oeuvres qui déroutaient toutes les notions traditionnelles de l'art en général, de la peinture en particulier."

Williams and Kreymborg were among the poets who joined the artists at Arensberg's apartment. At the time of the Armory Show Arensberg had begun to collect the work of Duchamp, Picasso, Gleizes, and others. His interests were wide-ranging, and he had published some books of poetry of a rather conventional kind. But after 1913 he began to write more and more freely, in some cases breaking up his lines in ways reminiscent of Mallarmé's "Un Coup de Dés" and occasionally using his poems as vehicles of philosophic disquisition on the theories of modern art. Arensberg, especially after he had come to know such men as Duchamp and Gleizes, became quite an authority on the new art. His apartment on Sixty-Seventh Street was a meeting place for anyone interested in art. "There were parties, mostly of paint-

[50] *Aires Abstraites*, 161-63.

ers, at Arensberg's studio," Williams recalled later: "These were of a different sort from the usual 'broke' goings on. Arensberg could afford to spread a really ample feed with drinks to match. You always saw Marcel Duchamp there. His painting on glass ['La Mariée Mise à Nu Par Ses Célibataires Même'], half-finished, stood at one side and several of his earlier works were on the wall, along with one of Cézanne's 'Woman Bathers,' the work of Gleizes and several others. It disturbed and fascinated me. I confess I was slow to come up with any answers."[51]

Duchamp was held in awe by most of the Americans; he was considered to be very much an intellectual giant. When once, in passing, he coolly rebuked Williams, who had had the audacity to comment on one of his paintings, the poet's self-esteem was hurt to the core. Duchamp was "parfaitement adapté au rythme violent de New York,"[52] and every one of his "anti-artistic" acts was considered further proof of his genius. A frequent topic of discussion was his concept of the "ready-made." This could be any everyday object that he, through his act of selection, made into a work of art. Duchamp had begun to collect such objects in 1913 in France, but he developed the implications of this notion fully only after he had settled in New York.

While the actions and the art of the expatriate contingent remained the subject of lunchtime colloquies between Arensberg, Williams, and others,[53] there continued to be numerous parties at which the intellect graciously yielded to more unbridled passions. In his

[51] Williams, *Autobiography*, 136.

[52] Buffet-Picabia, *Aires Abstraites*, 164.

[53] See the Introduction to Williams' *Kora in Hell: Improvisations* (Boston 1920), reprinted in his *Selected Essays* (New York 1954).

Autobiography Williams describes one at which "a French girl, of say eighteen or less" was courted in a rather intimate fashion by a number of young men at the same time. "She was in a black lace gown, fully at ease. It was something I had not seen before. Her feet were being kissed, her shins, her knees, and even above the knees, though as far as I could tell there was a gentleman's agreement that she was not to be undressed there."[54] In the spring of 1916 Williams himself gave a party that lasted a full twenty-four hours. Among those attending were Arensberg, Duchamp, Gleizes, Kreymborg, Man Ray, and Maxwell Bodenheim.

Notwithstanding the parties, or perhaps because of them, the painters, as well as the writers, continued to develop their art. "What were we [writers] seeking?" Williams reflected: "No one knew consistently enough to formulate a 'movement.' We were restless and constrained, closely allied with the painters."[55]

During April 1917 a large "Independents Exhibition" of painting was organized in New York. There were to be no prejudices in the selection of the exhibits; everyone was to have a chance. Duchamp, himself one of the organizers, but skeptical about the objectivity of the exhibition committee, sent in a urinal, which he called "Fountain" and signed "R. Mutt."[56] It was thrown out,

[54] *Autobiography*, 141.

[55] *Ibid.*, 148.

[56] This is most likely the exhibition at which Williams read his "Overture to a Dance of Locomotives" and "Portrait of a Woman in Bed." In his *Autobiography*, Williams associates this occasion vaguely with the Armory Show, and in his "Recollections" in *Art in America* he does so definitely. But in his *Autobiography* he also places the episode of the urinal at the Armory Show, and the two poems which he lists as having read, particularly the "Overture," were clearly not among his earliest work. The "Overture" was first published in *Sour Grapes* (1921), the "Portrait" in *Al Que Quiere* (1917).

35

as Duchamp had undoubtedly expected it would be, and became immediately a *cause célèbre* for the avant garde. Stieglitz made a photograph of the "Fountain" which was published in the second issue of *The Blind Man*, a magazine published by Henri Pierre Roché, and edited largely by Duchamp. Charles Demuth contributed a poem "For Richard Mutt," and the magazine editorialized: "Whether Mr. Mutt with his own hands made the fountain or not has no importance. He CHOSE it. He took an ordinary article of life, placed it so that its useful significance disappeared under the new title and point of view—created a new thought for that object."[57]

Duchamp was not the only one who created a scandal at the Independents Exhibition. Another was Arthur Cravan, an English poet who had lived mostly in France. Cravan had a singular talent for *épater* not only *les bourgeois* but also his fellow artists. He delighted in shocking others with his presumed brutality. One of his *bon mots* was that he would "rather practice indecency with a professor of philosophy at the Collège de France —*Monsieur Bergson* for instance—than go to bed with most Russian women."[58] In Barcelona he had recently fought the world champion boxer of that period, Jack Johnson. When he discussed painters, as he had done in his scurrilous pamphlet about the 1914 Paris Independents Exhibition, he was sure to be offensive.

Hoping for a scandal, the Picabia-Duchamp circle arranged for Cravan to give a lecture on modern art at the Independents, before an audience consisting mainly of society ladies and retired gentlemen, who wished to

[57] *The Blind Man*, I, 2 (May 1917), 5.
[58] Arthur Cravan, "Exhibition at the Independents," in Robert Motherwell, ed., *The Dada Painters and Poets* (New York 1951). Article reprinted from *Maintenant* (a magazine written and published by Cravan in Paris, 1913-1915).

be introduced into the mysteries of modern art. Cravan arrived drunk, and had hardly begun his "lecture" after stumbling to the podium when, to the dismay of the audience, he began to take off his clothes. Before he could go too far, however, the police intervened and Cravan was arrested. Arensberg managed to have him released, and no charges were pressed. Notwithstanding his actions, Cravan appears to have been a sensitive person, whose sense of the absurd was merely more consistent, and far less egotistically inclined than that of Duchamp or Picabia, and hence much more self-destructive. Mina Loy, whom he later married, easily preferred his attentions to those of a hesitant sinner such as Williams, who was furtively in love with her but who speedily recognized the futility of trying to compete with Cravan.[59]

Mina Loy, a remarkable and for that time impressively emancipated woman, was one of the major links between the New York avant garde and the Futurist movement in Europe. Before the start of the First World War she had met Marinetti and his group in Milan, and in Paris she had known Apollinaire. In New York she quickly became a source of admiration and wonder to timid American males. Both Kreymborg and Williams remembered vividly in later days how much they had been impressed by her poems for *Others*, with their stark, uncompromising imagery. As a person she was generally considered the perfect foil to Marianne Moore, whose "austerity of mood," according to Williams, more than balanced Mina's intensity. "Of all those writing poetry in America at the time she was here Marianne Moore was the only one Mina Loy feared. By divergent virtues these two women have achieved freshness of presenta-

[59] Williams mutilates Cravan's name in his *Autobiography* as well as in some of his other writings. calling him "John Craven."

37

tion, novelty, freedom, break with banality," Williams wrote in the Prologue to *Kora in Hell*.

During 1917 three magazines were published in New York which now figure prominently among the documents of the Dada movement: *391*, *The Blind Man*, and *Rongwrong*.

A few months after 291 stopped publishing, in August 1916, Picabia left the United States and went to Barcelona, where he lived for some time among a contingent of Parisian *émigrés* similar to that in New York. There he decided to start a magazine based on 291. His sense of consistency told him that it should be called 391, for, as Michel Sanouillet has remarked, the first issue was "calquée sans vergogne sur le dernier numéro de 291."[60] Four issues of 391 appeared in Barcelona. Then, in March 1917, Picabia returned to New York, but he continued to publish 391. The New York issues contained contributions by Arensberg, De Zayas, Gleizes, Edgar Varèse, and, of course, Picabia himself. Three issues appeared, which undoubtedly had a great currency among the people around Stieglitz, Duchamp, and Arensberg. After these three issues 391 disappears, until in 1919, together with Picabia, it makes its reappearance among the Dadaists in Zurich (Plate III).

The Blind Man and *Rongwrong*, both edited by Marcel Duchamp, contained contributions from the same small group around Stieglitz and Arensberg. In fact, a chess game which took place between Picabia and Henri Pierre Roché figures in both 391 and *Rongwrong*. Among the contributors to Duchamp's magazines were Mina Loy, Carl Van Vechten, Stieglitz, and Charles Duncan, and there were reproductions of paintings by Eilshemius, Joseph Stella, and John Covert.

[60] Michel Sanouillet, "Francis Picabia et *391*," introduction to integral reissue of 391 (Paris, Le Terrain Vague, 1960), 8-16.

In the first issue of *The Blind Man* Henry Pierre Roché, in an editorial to "the American Public," mentions in passing that "your 'little theatre' movement has come." And, indeed, in MacDougall Street the Provincetown Players were beginning to perform some of Eugene O'Neill's first plays. Among those who caught the playwriting virus were Kreymborg and Williams. The Provincetown Players allowed them to use their stage for their attempts at drama, and a performance of a play called *Lima Beans*, by Kreymborg, was a modest success. The parts in it were acted by William Carlos Williams, Mina Loy, and William Zorach, the sculptor. Gleizes, Duchamp, and Stieglitz were in the audience.

In the meantime the number of artists frequenting 291 had continued to expand steadily. Among those who had more recently begun to venture into the tiny elevator to be lifted to "the Attic near the Roof," as Djuna Barnes called it,[61] were Charles Sheeler, Waldo Frank, Paul Rosenfeld, Sherwood Anderson, Stanton Macdonald Wright, and Carl Sandburg. Charles Demuth has recorded vividly how among artists a visit to 291 could mean a renewed acquaintance with the work of Picasso, Kandinsky, or any of a number of major new painters. Stieglitz had begun to assemble a large private collection of key works of the modern movement, and he was willing to show any of these works to his acquaintances, when asked. At the same time the walls of the gallery itself might be "emotionally hung with African carvings, there was also yellow and orange and black; yellow, orange, black. There were photographs of African carvings. There was a photograph of two hands. *That was a moment.*"[62] To Marianne Moore, 291 was "an

[61] *Camera Work*, 47 (July 1914; published January 1915).
[62] Charles Demuth, "Between Four and Five," *Camera Work*, 47 (January 1915).

American Acropolis so to speak, with a stove in it, a kind of eagle's perch of selectiveness, and like the ardor of fire in its completeness."[63]

Among the exhibitions at 291 there continued to be many "firsts." Oscar Bluemner had his first one-man show there in 1915, as did Elie Nadelman. Every year there was a Marin exhibition, and Marsden Hartley also continued to have shows from time to time. In May 1916 Stieglitz showed some watercolors by Georgia O'Keeffe, a young lady whose work baffled the press. But Stieglitz knew that he had finally found a woman who could paint, or for that matter, as it would turn out, a woman whom he could photograph, with fascinating precision, for decades to come.

In 1917 Stieglitz showed more of O'Keeffe's work, as well as that of Walkowitz, Gino Severini, and Stanton Macdonald Wright. As had been the case during the Armory Show, when Stieglitz hung a large selection of his photographs, 291 returned to its original purpose during the Forum Exhibition of American Art of 1916, with a comprehensive show of photography by Paul Strand. Stieglitz, who considered Strand the first true photographer in many years, even revived *Camera Work* for one issue, so that some of Strand's photography could be studied and kept at hand by those who realized its significance. Although *Camera Work* was officially dead, another magazine had come to take its place, *The Seven Arts*, a magazine which was in many ways an amplification of what Stieglitz stood for. In the first of its few issues, Paul Rosenfeld wrote a glowing tribute to Stieglitz and 291: "Only to those who seek the gallery at a moment when the individual staying power is near col-

[63] Marianne Moore, "Stieglitz," in *Stieglitz Memorial Portfolio, 1864-1946*, ed. by Dorothy Norman (New York, Twice a Year Press 1947).

lapse, when energy subsides and faith crumbles and vanishes, does it reveal itself. . . . What matter who is being shown there, Matisse or Picabia or Walkowitz? What matter whether you are astonished or ravished or appalled? What matter so long as you feel their revolt, their daring, their fearless self-expression. These are the great venturers. These are the artists who have abandoned dead conventionality, renounced smug repetition of other men's thoughts, to find themselves. These are the men who have discarded representation in order to creep the closer to life, and get some of its naked rhythm onto their canvas or into their marble. Their art has it in its power to give you what only a thing made in your own time, under the conditions imposed by your own time, out of the fabric of your own time, can give you." Rosenfeld concludes: "But one thing counts here. It is the courage to realize yourself, to express yourself, to shape your life as you would. No half-measures, no compromise. No timid withholding."[64]

In a later issue Paul Strand emphasized that aside from its role as a center for artists and writers, 291 had another perhaps even greater significance: Through *Camera Work* and Stieglitz's photography, "America has really been expressed in terms of America, without the outside influence of Paris art-schools or their dilute offspring."[65]

But things were changing. America had abandoned its precarious neutrality and had entered into the war. A deadly seriousness began to take hold of the American public; a war mentality set in. The seemingly carefree, irreverent artists who had been tolerated by the public at large, and had even figured in many a good-natured

[64] Paul Rosenfeld (Peter Minuit), "291 Fifth Avenue," *The Seven Arts* (November 1916), 61-65.
[65] Paul Strand, "Photography," *The Seven Arts* (August 1917), 524-26.

exposé of modern art as examples of amiable frauds, began to find the atmosphere more and more oppressive. The freedom of thought and action they had enjoyed in New York became an "illusion vite dissipée."[66] The international contingent of the avant garde began to disperse. Picabia and his wife returned to Europe, others went to South America. Arthur Cravan and Mina Loy went to Mexico and got married. Then Mina continued on to Buenos Aires, where Cravan was to join her. He had fitted out a small yacht on which he hoped to sail down along the coast. But somehow, somewhere, through accident or through his own determination, he disappeared forever. Duchamp first went to Buenos Aires, then, like most of the others, back to Paris.

The Seven Arts folded. Its integrity and the unpopular anti-war views of its editors, especially Randolph Bourne, were its death-warrant. Some of the younger Americans who had just begun to have a taste of what "artistic life" could be like, now joined the army, and were to rediscover many of the artists they had held most in awe, in Paris after the war. But by that time things had happened in the literary world which took it out of the shadow of painting and gave it an avant garde entirely of its own. In the United States there remained more of a contact between artists and writers than there had been before the Armory Show, but there was never again to be such close integration as there had been during the few years before America's entry into the war. In 1946, Duchamp, reminiscing about those years, said: "During the other war [1914-1919] life among the artists in New York was quite different—much more congenial than it has been in these last few years. Among the artists there was much more cohesion—much closer fel-

[66] Buffet-Picabia, *Aires Abstraites*, 161.

lowship, much less opportunism. The whole spirit was
much different. There was quite a bit of activity, but it
was limited to a relatively small group and nothing was
done very publicly. Publicity always takes something
away. And the great advantage in that earlier period was
that the art of the time was laboratory work; now it is
diluted for public consumption."[67]

Perhaps the most striking of the casualties of the war
was 291. The changed attitude of the public and rising
costs forced Stieglitz to close his laboratory. Sadly dis-
illusioned with the turn of events, he was doubtful that
he would ever venture into public life again. He did not
know that his career as a public figure had just begun,
and would reach into the mid-1940's, bringing him in
touch with most of the major figures in American cultural life. Already his role had been seminal. For nearly
ten years he had given the young, the daring, and the
unconventional a shelter at 291. And although the very
fact that 291 was a gallery tended to emphasize its role
as a center for painters, Stieglitz himself cared only about
the sincerity of an artist's endeavors, in whatever medium
he was trying to express himself. "He always gave freely
and without strings attached," Guido Bruno said in his
obituary of 291: "If poets published their poetry, he
subscribed for a good many copies; he bought pictures
from artists. The editors of individualistic magazines
came to him for their first subscriptions, and I don't
know of one instance where he tried to sell anything. . . .
There is not one name that I can think of among the
artists of the past fifteen years and among the writers as
well, who did not puzzle at one stage of his career about
Stieglitz's establishment."[68]

[67] Marcel Duchamp, *Marchand du Sel,* writings edited by
Michel Sanouillet (Paris, Le Terrain Vague 1958), 109.
[68] Bruno, "The Passing of 291."

Although 291 was closed, its fame had been so wide-spread that it created a legend among aspiring artists who had been too young to find their way to its door in time. One of these, Gorham Munson, remembers that for him 291 became a magic number representing creativity, so much so, in fact, that when in 1921 he sailed to Europe, he painted "291" on his trunk. He put the numerals on so that he might recognize his baggage at French and Italian railway stations, but, he said, "they were more magical than utilitarian to me."[69]

In the meantime writers like Williams Carlos Williams or Wallace Stevens did of course not find themselves suddenly without a place to go. The contrary was true. *The Little Review* was coming into prominence as a controversial voice of the avant garde, and the scene of parties merely shifted to apartments in Greenwich Village, such as that of Lola Ridge. But the aspect of these meetings and parties had changed. Painters still joined in with the writers, but the gatherings became predominantly literary. The sense of excitement and experiment, which had had its origin in the activities of the painters, was more than ever channeled into literature. In the festive atmosphere of new discovery, the generative role of the painters was forgotten, especially since Dada and Surrealism, as they began to manifest themselves in Paris, seemed to be at least as much the discovery of writers as of painters. Moreover, budding avant gardists who had been either too young to have witnessed the years between 1913 and 1917, or had been in the "provinces" ambitiously sending their imagist poems to *Poetry*, unaware of what was happening in New York, were now invading Greenwich Village. To all these the activity of the avant garde seemed part of

[69] Gorham Munson, " '291': A Creative Source of the Twenties," *Forum*, III (Fall-Winter 1960), 4-9.

an indigenous literary movement. Thus Gorham Munson, who had heard so much of 291, could freely assert that "291 was a creative source of the 'Twenties,'" and that "creative vitality stemmed from it throughout the period," but at the same time doubt that it had significant influence on literature.[70]

The foregoing account of what was happening among the members of an admittedly small group of avant garde artists in New York during the 1910's reveals that there is good reason to assume that 291, as well as painting in general, had a potent influence on the poets in that group. People such as Williams, who had been so strongly attracted to painting from his early youth, were clearly especially susceptible to what was happening in painting.

It should be emphasized, however, that although the "Roaring Twenties" may have started as early as 1913 for this small group of artists, the activities of the group were, as Duchamp said, not generally publicized. The forces of the "establishment," in both art and literature, regarded their activity as that of an unimportant lunatic fringe. Nor was the literary community which formed around *Poetry, The Little Review,* and its expatriate guidance counselor Ezra Pound, especially in Chicago, affected to any large extent by what was happening in New York at that time. What the foregoing account does show, however, is that the influence of Imagism; *Poetry,* and Pound was far less pervasive than it is generally made out to be, especially where poets such as Williams, Wallace Stevens, and Marianne Moore are concerned. A close study of the early writings of these poets cannot be possible without a thorough investigation of the sources presented by the visual arts of that time.

[70] *Ibid.*

For Williams in particular this period was of crucial importance, and, as I intend to show, his development as a poet was in fact determined by his pervasive interest in the visual arts.

II. THE POEM AS A CANVAS
OF BROKEN PARTS

*t*HE EARLIEST published poems of William Carlos
Williams are hardly indicative of the independent direction his later work was to take. His privately printed
Poems (1909) is made up of inept attempts at poetry in
the manner of Keats and Shakespeare. It is a pretentious
collection of ballads, odes to Innocence, and apostrophes
to the seasons, all equally artificial. To Williams these
poems remained, during his later years, a source of fond
embarrassment, but at the time of their initial appearance in print he was filled with pride over lines such as
"Of youth himself all rose-yclad."[1] It is tempting to dismiss these poems as juvenilia, representative of a budding poet's early follies and imitative enthusiasms. But
these *Poems* were far from being the exercises of an ado-
lescent. In 1909 Williams was twenty six, and he had
already shown a profound interest in poetry for nearly
a decade.[2]

The early work of important poets is likely to contain
some indications of the qualities which will find full
expression in their mature work. In Williams' *Poems*
these indications are absent. The themes of the poems
may suggest that to some extent the poet was "stating
[his] case right from the beginning,"[3] but in terms of
style they offer hardly a hint of what was to come, and as
Williams himself frequently emphasized, "it is not what
you say that matters but the manner in which you
say it."[4]

[1] *I Wanted To Write a Poem*, 10.
[2] *Ibid.*, 1-4.
[3] *Ibid.*, 9.
[4] Williams, *Selected Essays*, xii.

47

During the years 1909-1910 Willaims studied in Europe, and in 1910 he visited Ezra Pound in London. Pound introduced him to the "intense literary atmosphere"[5] of the British capital. After that visit to his old college acquaintance, Williams' poetry began to change. He now used Poundian hortative and exclamatory phrases, his language became more colloquial, and he added what he must have thought were "clever" literary allusions. When Pound officially adopted Imagism, Williams unhesitatingly followed. *The Tempers* (1913), Williams' first commercially published book, placed by Pound with Elkin Matthews in London, is remarkable only for Williams' faithful pursuit of Pound's stylistic example. Williams even went so far as to write imitations of the work of such poets as Browning, advocated by Pound as proper models. Williams, however, lacked Pound's literary sophistication, his diction was simpler, and his images were those of sea, sky, garden, and forest. The themes, again, are close to Williams' later concerns, but in terms of style these poems are very largely derivative.

From 1913 on, however, the direct influence of Pound and what might be called "orthodox" Imagism on Williams diminished rapidly. Other literary influences took their place, such as the work of Alfred Kreymborg, Maxwell Bodenheim, and Mina Loy. Soon Williams' poetry began to take its own form, and by the end of 1915 he was easily the least understood poet in what was then called the "*Others* Group."

Thus Williams, who had been a derivative poet up to at least the age of thirty, became within a few years a remarkably original one. The reasons for this striking transformation have never been adequately discussed. It

[5] Williams, *Autobiography*, 117.

is generally assumed that the change was due to the progressive maturation of Williams' poetic skills. This factor
certainly comes into play, but Williams had been writing
for nearly fifteen years when the change began to occur,
a rather long novitiate. He had not shown any decided
propensity toward stylistic originality, and it seems
unlikely that he would have at a later date, had he
remained within the purely literary concerns of the
1910's. It was Williams' interest in the visual arts, and his
fascinated immersion in the experimental activities of
the painters in New York during those years, which determined him to find his own style. It is therefore not
surprising that the kind of poetic notation which he
developed was profoundly influenced by the visual qualities of the new art, and by the theories which had been
created to explain it.

To some extent Williams' special concern for painting
had influenced the iconography of his poems from the
beginning. Recalling his attempts at writing a Keatsian
epic while he was still at college, Williams describes how
at one point in the opus there occurred "a secondary
dream, the scene of which was, deliberately, Boecklin's
'Insel des 'I'odes,' which I knew from a cheap print I
had seen somewhere or other. The prince saw himself
transported to that dire place in a boat—but at this point
the poem bogged down."[6] Botticelli's "Birth of Venus"
is a recurring visitor to Williams' poems, from *The Tempers* to *Paterson*. But until at least 1913 Williams' poetry
was in large part based stylistically on literary precedent.
The visual shock of the Armory Show, and the hectic
painter-dominated years that followed, made it possible
for him to reformulate his means of expression in terms
of the stylistic concepts of these painters. Their newly

[6] *Ibid.*, 59.

49

developed theories about the visual reconstruction of reality on canvas became the basis for Williams' method. It should be emphasized, however, that Williams was largely an intuitive poet and, at least at this stage in his career, not much given to theorizing. It is therefore likely that his earliest moves towards the transposition of painterly techniques to poetry were based on only a vague determination to do for poetry what the painters had done for painting. As Williams' personal style developed, the full nature of his debt to the visual arts in the construction of his poems probably remained hidden even to him, but he knew that his work had a close affinity to what the painters were doing, and he never tried to hide his awareness of their importance to his development as a poet.

Imagism showed Williams the need for a clearly developed, sharply delineated image, and Imagism made him realize that the rhythms and patterns of rhyme which his older contemporaries were using were burdens to be discarded. But the individuality and iconoclasm of the painters who exhibited at the Armory Show, their lack of respect for what had seemed to be the most basic laws of pictorial art, their manifestoes in 291, and the protodada activities of Duchamp and Picabia—those were the elements which convinced Williams that he should take a step which the Imagists had failed to take, because they were too staid or because they lacked the intense visual orientation usually associated with painters. The step Williams took consisted of a "progression from the concept, the thought, to the poem itself," just as "the painters following Cézanne began to talk of sheer paint: a picture a matter of pigments upon a piece of cloth stretched on a frame." It is the making of that step, Williams remarks in the closing pages of his *Autobiography*,

"to come over into the tactile qualities, the words themselves beyond the mere thought expressed that distin-
guishes the modern, or distinguished the modern of that
time from the period before the turn of the century. And
it is the reason why painting and the poem became so
closely allied at that time. It was the work of the painters following Cézanne and the Impressionists that, criti-
cally, opened up the age of Stein, Joyce and a good many
others."[7]

The step from the concept to the thing itself, from
"feeling to the imaginative object," from the image as
metaphor to the image as subject, was one of the first
Williams took on the path which led him away from
Imagism and into his lifelong attempt to transpose the
visual space and the tensions of painting to the realm of
poetry. In Imagist poems the image is usually a metaphor reconstituting an experience in terms of a pictorial
equivalent. "These faces in the crowd" are "petals on a
wet, black bough." Thus an Imagist poem, although pictorial in its conception, is essentially a literary fragment,
not a unit such as a painting or any other tactile object.
It is part of a sequential enumeration of emotive simili-
tudes. If a painter attempts to introduce sequential
effects of this kind into his work, the effect is nearly
always "literary": the painting becomes anecdotal, the
viewer feels the strain of the narrative content, the
"story" takes precedent over the visual construct.
Sequence has, on the other hand, always been one of the
primary tools of the verbal artist, who has used this
device, and still uses it, nearly continuously, but who in
its employment must sacrifice the immediacy and objective concentration available to the painter.

Williams' poetry begins to diverge significantly from

[7] *Ibid.*, 380.

the Imagist examples from 1915 onward. There is a progressive tendency for the image to become subject rather than metaphor. The image no longer has to represent something else; it becomes self-supporting. It ceases to be agent and it becomes topic. The parts of the poem become a record of the poet's subjective perception of the field of visual experience represented by the image which constitutes the poem. This is of course exactly the procedure of the visual artist, who records his visual experience—be it direct, reconstructed, or imagined—as he perceives it, within the visual space of his construction.

In a process of this kind the first aspect of conventional literary usage to be discarded is the narrative sequence within the poem, which even more than metaphor obstructs the immediacy of a poem's impact. In Williams' poetry the abandonment of narrative sequence begins to occur soon after the publication of *The Tempers* and becomes nearly complete in poems such as "Dawn," "Spring Strains," "Winter Quiet," and "A Portrait in Greys," from *Al Que Quiere* (1917). These poems are all clearly delineated "pictures" in which the action occurs within the limits of a visual plane and within an instant of perception, removed from nearly all sense of temporal progression and consequently without a clearly defined narrative sequence. Williams' move toward the elimination of narrative sequence was quite premeditated. Much later, commenting on the popularity of his poem "Tract," which originally appeared in *Others* in 1916, at a time when even his closest literary friends were beginning to look askance at him, he said it probably became a favorite "because it has almost a narrative sequence."[8]

A painting represents a moment of perception. It con-

---

[8] *I Wanted To Write a Poem*, 25.

sists of a field of experience made instantaneously perceptible. It is a moment in time, suspended and lifted outside the sequence of time, rescued as it were for eternity. Bad painting selects an aspect of reality, isolates it, and reproduces it on canvas accurately and precisely, or does so clumsily and inaccurately, reducing the original to something less than its reality. In Williams' words, it "copies." Good painting, however, again using Williams' terminology, "imitates" nature. That is, in selecting, isolating, and reproducing an aspect of reality, the artist distills its essence and intensifies it by stripping from it all details which might obstruct the purity of the experience, concentrating entirely on the elements which enhance its meaning. The immediacy of a painting's impact, due to the precise delineation of its visual space, and the potential intensity of its recorded experience, as well as its position outside the progress of time, are the qualities which Williams admired most in the painter's art. He soon began to consider these qualities essential to the kind of poetry he wished to write, for "all things enter into the singleness of the moment and the moment partakes of the diversity of all things."[9]

Williams believed that the quality of an artist's work is dependent upon the accuracy with which he manages to record the workings of his creative imagination. "To take to the imagination is the first prerequisite for creation."[10] Williams conceived of the imagination as a condition analogous to the undetermined moments between waking and sleeping, when the mind breaks up, rearranges and then fixes the images which it has collected—the picture units of experience—as if they were photo-montages on the film of memory. These picture

---

[9] *Selected Essays*, 97.
[10] *Ibid.*, 307.

units have the same power as photographs or paintings to suspend a moment of intense action forever, to be analyzed, looked at, or glanced over. The action represented by the original event has been caught, and because of that continues forever—but outside of the destructive power of time, for "time is a storm in which we are all lost."[11] The non-sequential visual unit thus fixed and projected on the mind retains its qualities of movement. It rather than time becomes the field of action, breaking the stiffness of the original image, moving within the framework of its limits: "We look at the ceiling and review the fixities of the day, the month, the year, the lifetime. Then it begins; that happy time when the image becomes broken or begins to break up, becomes a little fluid—or is affected, floats brokenly in the fluid. The rigidities yield—like ice in March, the magic month."[12] Finally the parts of the image once more coalesce and become "that veritable fusion of objects within a restricted space" which Albert Gleizes and Jean Metzinger considered the definition of a good painting,[13] and which Williams saw as the basis for the construction of an effective poem. To create his work of art, the artist records the visual unit established by means of this process with whatever technical means he has at his disposal. "I'm trying to get a particular effect," Williams once said in an interview, "like some kinds of modern painting. . . . That's the way I've always tried to work."[14]

[11] *Ibid.*, xvi.
[12] *Ibid.*, 307.
[13] Albert Gleizes and Jean Metzinger, "Cubism" (1912), in *Modern Artists on Art*, ed. Robert L. Herbert (Englewood Cliffs 1964), 5.
[14] Quoted in John C. Thirlwall, "William Carlos Williams' 'Paterson,' The Search for the Redeeming Language," *New Directions*, 17 (New York 1961), 252-310.

Williams' description of the imagination at work is clearly indebted to early explanations of the procedure that produced Cubism and the other forms of pictorial art which were breaking away from orthodox visual representation in the beginning of the twentieth century. It is likely that he originally formulated this concept of the function of the imagination only after he had become familiar with the new art and had begun to try to emulate it in poetry. Williams, indeed, always had a tendency towards the almost literal transference to literature of visual effects used in painting; during these attempts he would gradually develop a viable compromise between the demands of language and his urge to paint with words. Williams' theories of poetry and of art in general can be traced directly to their origin in the methods and attitudes prevalent among the painters with whom and with whose work he became familiar during the 1910's and after. Thus Williams' urge to "make it new" finds its origin in his observation of and admiration for such painters as Marcel Duchamp. In the "Prologue" to *Kora in Hell* he records how in discussions with Walter Conrad Arensberg about the art of these painters he learned that "the only way man differed from every other creature was in his ability to improvise novelty and, since the pictorial artist was under discussion, anything in paint that is truly new, truly a fresh creation, is good art."[15]

Part of Williams' restlessness within the traditional framework of literature, therefore, and his attempts at keeping pace with the discoveries of the painters, stem from the belief which he had adopted on their authority,

[15] *Selected Essays*, 5. Williams first published the "Prologue" in *The Little Review* (April, May 1919) and reprinted it, with some omissions, in *Kora in Hell* (1920). It was subsequently included in his *Selected Essays*.

that "nothing is good save the new. If a thing have novelty it stands intrinsically beside every other work of artistic excellence. If it have not that, no loveliness or heroic proportion or grand manner will save it."[16] Clearly the urge for novelty and the unusual which is so largely a feature of Williams' poetry and which aligns his work not infrequently with that of the Dadaists in spirit, stems from this source. In view of the closeness of Williams' association with the activities of the New York avant garde, as outlined in the previous chapter, this is certainly not surprising. These influences seem to have supplied the energy for Williams' continued efforts throughout his life to find a "new measure."

After the year of *The Tempers* and the Armory Show Williams became for some time closely associated with Alfred Kreymborg, a poet with a great deal of enthusiasm for new causes. Kreymborg's poetry, under the influence of his experiences at 291 itself largely determined in form by the new painting, had developed into a record of homely observation, farm-boy language, and childish bits of sentimental wonder about the "objects" we encounter in our daily lives:

> EVERY MORNING
> Our halls are very dark.
> But not so dark we cannot see,
> every morning,
> a bent old figure,
> kneeling,
> on the steps or in the halls,
>   scrubbing—
> what you call a janitress.
> Good morning, she says.
> Good morning, say we.

[16] *Selected Essays*, 21.

Our halls are very dark,
but not so dark—[17]

Poems such as this undoubtedly helped Williams to get rid of the "classic" poetic diction which afflicted his earliest poems. The series of "my townspeople" poems ("Tract," "Invitation," "Gulls," and others) which Williams wrote around 1914-1915 combine the colloquial exuberance derived from Pound with the colloquial homeliness of Kreymborg. But Kreymborg, Williams decided early, was not a good example to follow. He soon began to feel that Kreymborg's poetry failed because it had "little help from the eyes."[18] The eyes, the source of all visual art, were to be Williams' guide. Poems such as "Pastoral," "Metric Figure," and "Chicory and Daisies," published in 1915, clearly show the development of Williams' painterly approach. "Metric Figure," for instance, does not have a narrative sequence, and describes a visual unit which can be sharply delineated and lifted outside the movement of time:

There is a bird in the poplars!
It is the sun!
The leaves are little yellow fish
swimming in the river.
The bird skims above them,
day is on his wings.
Phoebus!
It is he that is making
the great gleam among the poplars!
It is his singing
outshines the noise
of leaves clashing in the wind.

[17] Alfred Kreymborg, *Mushrooms* (New York 1916), 44.
[18] William Carlos Williams, "Prologue, Part II," *The Little Review*, VI, 1 (May 1919), 75. The passage containing this remark was not reprinted in *Kora in Hell*.

As we read the poem we discover the details of the "painting": The "bird in the poplars" on closer look becomes the sun; what seem "little yellow fish" are leaves. Thus we see how the metaphor of Imagism has been reduced to a painterly *trompe l'oeil* which fits properly into the visual space of the poem. Williams has moved from the literary concept to the visual "thing." "I was interested in the construction of an image [instead of the use of imagistic concepts within the larger framework of a narrative poem] before the image was popular in poetry. The poem 'Metric Figure' is an example. I was influenced by my mother's still lifes."[19]

Williams' new concern for the "thing," for the image as subject, for the poem which depicts rather than philosophizes, the poem in which meaning is determined by the visual presentation of the subject rather than by literary reflection, is also clearly represented in his "Chicory and Daisies," where he attempts to depict in completely visual terms the struggle of the flower against the odds nature has thrown in its way. In this poem the poet still seeks some recourse to extraneous (literary) commentary ("scorn greyness," "the sky goes out/ if you should fail"), but Williams was very clear about his intention: "A poet witnessing the chicory flower and realizing its virtues of form and color so constructs his praise of it as to borrow no particle from right or left. He gives his poem over to the flower and its plant themselves, that they may benefit by those cooling winds of the imagination which thus returned upon them will refresh them at their task of saving the world."[20]

Williams' concern for the object per se, was, as has been shown, a necessary and logical correlative to his attempts at approximating the visual and emotional

[19] I *Wanted To Write a Poem*, 21.
[20] *Selected Essays*, 17.

unity of painting in poetry. But he could not have come to his awareness of the intrinsic significance of the object through a study of the conventional art of the 1910's, which was rigorously anecdotal. It was Cézanne, the Cubists, and the Futurists who called Williams' attention to the object, for they and their American followers, "instead of concentrating on the atmosphere," concentrated on form. In them "there is an attempt to render plastic the inner constitution of objects."[21] From them he learned that "moving around an object to seize from it several successive appearances, which fused into a single image, reconstitute it in time," must be a major concern of the new artist,[22] for any picture in which the spectator is invited to "follow the story" would reduce its emotional intensity. "We must therfore find a form which excludes a fairy-tale effect and which does not hinder pure color action. To this end, form, movement, color, natural and imaginary objects must be divorced from any narrative intent."[23] If all this had not been sufficient to kindle Williams' awareness of the importance of the object in art there would always have been Duchamp to startle him with his "Ready-mades."

But Williams learned quickly, and soon was confident enough about the success of his new-found stylistic approximation of painting to become didactic about his procedure. In 1916, in "To a Solitary Disciple," he preaches the importance of making the parts of the poem visual units rather than "poetic" conceits. It is more important, he says, to tell

[21] Hutchins Hapgood in *Camera Work*, xxxviii (April 1912), 43.
[22] Gleizes and Metzinger, *op.cit.*, 15.
[23] Wassily Kandinsky, *The Spiritual in Art* (1912) (George Wittenborn & Co., *The Documents of Modern Art*, New York 1947), 71.

59

> that the moon is
> tilted above
> the point of the steeple
> than that its color
> is shell-pink.

Do not include metaphors which obstruct the immediacy of the poetic experience:

> Rather observe
> that it is early morning
> than that the sky
> is smooth
> as a turquoise.

The long poem "March," which was published in the October 1916 issue of *The Egoist*, comes close to being a manifesto. March is the "magic month" of rebirth, and reminds the poet of great works of art in history which were representative of a rebirth of creativity, such as the ancient reliefs of "Ashur-ban-i-pal/the archer king" and Fra Angelico's fresco of the Annunciation.[24] These two works represent earlier springtimes of the imagination which Williams relives and assimilates, for in his awareness of their visual power "they are coming into bloom again!" making him ready to become the leader of the "band of / young poets that have not learned / the blessedness of warmth / (or have forgotten it)," and who will have to battle their way towards the "third springtime." Williams, "seeking one flower" in which to warm himself, urges them not to give in, but to "think of the painted monastery / at Fiesole," which contains the answer to their search for form.

But "March" is remarkable for more than its signifi-

---

[24] Williams is mistaken in locating the fresco at Fiesole. It is in the convent of San Marco in Florence.

cance as a manifesto. Williams' visual evocation of
"Ashur-ban-i-pal, / the archer king on horseback," based
as it is on an existing work of art, is in itself a curious
example of the synthesizing process of his visual imagination, intensifying the qualities remembered from several
images—in this case the various episodes of the Great
Lion Hunt reliefs from the North Palace of king Ashurbanipal at Nineveh, in the British Museum. The scenes
of these reliefs are not "in blue and yellow enamel"; they
are carved in alabaster. Again, on the reliefs, when the
"king on horseback" dispatches a lion, he uses a lance;
when in other episodes he shoots arrows at lions he does
so from his chariot. The only time when he is actually
an "archer king on horseback" he is shooting wild asses,
not lions. Thus Williams' imagination has selected and
retained the most dramatic and visually exciting details
from the original reliefs and has rearranged them into
a more direct visual pattern, which intensifies into one
image the impact of an extensive sequence of related
reliefs. The "blue and yellow enamel" which Williams
erroneously ascribes to the Ashurbanipal reliefs actually
belong to an entirely different visual structure, namely
to the

> Sacred bulls—dragons
> in embossed brickwork
> marching—in four tiers—
> along the sacred way to
> Nebuchadnessar's throne hall!

Here Williams is referring to the magnificent bulls and
dragons in glazed brick which decorated the Ishtar Gate
of Babylon, and which are now in the Berlin Museum.
These "dragons with / upright tails and sacred bulls"
appeared indeed yellow on deep blue "enamelled walls,"
to those in "procession to / the god, Marduk." Williams,

61

in other words, has drawn a composite picture based on an extensive series of visual episodes, modified and unified by his imagination; in doing so he has managed with remarkable skill to convey the immediacy of the visual experience represented by the original works of art.

In "March" Williams also for the first time makes a poem out of an existing painting in the most literal sense, something he would continue to do frequently during the rest of his long career as a poet, until in his *Pictures from Brueghel* this became his major concern. In "March" he describes the Fra Angelico "Annunciation" as follows:

> My second spring—painted
> a virgin—in a blue aureole
> sitting on a three-legged stool,
> arms crossed—
> she is intently serious,
>   and still
> watching an angel
> with colored wings
> half kneeling before her—
> and smiling—the angel's eyes
> holding the eyes of Mary
> as a snake's hold a bird's.
> On the ground there are flowers,
> trees are in leaf.

This description set a pattern which Williams continued to follow faithfully in poems of this kind: he records the details of the image presented by the painting in the order of their visual importance—in the same order, in other words, in which, on seeing the painting, his awareness would register them. He does not embellish his description, except when he wishes to transmit certain aspects of mood in the painting which cannot be transformed directly into verbal objects. Thus the angel's eyes hold Mary's "as a snake's hold a bird's." The poetic unit which results is a part of the temporal process only insofar as reading is, but in those terms a painting is too— for it takes time to scrutinize a painting in detail. In all other respects the unit is outside the sequence of time in literature (narrative continuity), because, just as in a painting, the details can be examined in any order desired. In fact, the unit can be read sentence by sentence almost as effectively from the last line up to the first, without any real obstruction to its meaning. As Williams said: "This is a principle we can utilize to our profit in estimating the quality of any piece of writing: by reading it backward, paragraph by paragraph, from somewhere near the end back to the beginning and thus finishing. I find my own sensual pleasure greatly increased by so doing. I am much better able to judge of the force of the work in this way. Only after careful consideration can a work be fully appreciated when read glibly from start to finish—unless it be made expressly for no other purpose—to avoid a closer scrutiny."[25]

Although Williams continued to "transliterate" existing paintings into poems from time to time—as fingering exercises, one could say—he undoubtedly realized that this kind of activity was suspiciously close to the kind of "copying" he professed to abhor. Kandinsky in *The Spiritual in Art*, an essay with which Williams was almost certainly familiar at this time, while urging a closer relationship between the arts, had warned that "Comparison of means among the arts and the learning of one art from another can only be successful when the application of the lesson is fundamental. One art must learn

[25] William Carlos Williams, "What Is the Use of Poetry?" unpublished, undated, ms. in the Lockwood Memorial Library Poetry Collection, State University of New York at Buffalo.

how another uses its method, so that its own means may then be used according to the same fundamental principles, but in its own medium. The artist must not forget that each means implies its proper application, and that it is for him to discover this application."[26] Williams therefore concentrated on the theories behind the new art—on the revolutionary concepts which had brought it about, the new perception, the new consciousness of the object which it established—and tried to apply what he learned to his poetry, aware of the limitations imposed on his efforts by the essentially non-pictorial nature of language compared to the other representational arts. He conceived of his poems as physical units, as paintings, having as their borders the limits set by space and the instant of perception. He aimed at the instantaneity of impression and vision painting presents to the viewer, attempting to incorporate in his poems the compressive qualities which were such a major feature of the new art.

A number of poems in *Al Que Quiere*, probably mostly written towards the later part of 1916, are representative of Williams' new stylistic concerns. Among the most striking of these are "Winter Quiet," "Spring Strains," and "Conquest." "Spring Strains" is in fact an elaborate attempt at painting a Cubist picture in words. It represents a visual plane, a visual field of action, within which objects are analyzed in a strictly pictorial fashion. They are isolated, intensified through compression, then broken into parts:

> two blue-grey birds chasing
> a third struggle in circles, angles,
> swift convergings to a point that bursts
> instantly!

Williams shatters the forms in his picture just as a

[26] Kandinsky, *op.cit.*, 40.

Cubist painter fragments his forms, and in doing so he achieves the "constructive dispersal of these fragments over the canvas" of his poem which Kandinsky mentions in discussing the work of Picasso.[27] Yet the poem contains far more movement than a Cubist work by Picasso; in this respect it uncannily resembles certain paintings of Franz Marc, a painter far closer in spirit to Williams than Picasso. The flashing, pulling, and straining lines formed by trees, buds, twigs, sky, and sun in Williams' poem effectively conjure up Franz Marc's painting "Tirol" (Plate iv). It is possible that Williams had seen a reproduction of this painting, but that is neither likely nor of much importance. The similarity in concept between the poem and the painting stems rather from the fact that Williams and Marc had been influenced by common sources: the work of Picasso and Kandinsky, agitated by the vehemence of the Futurists:

(Hold hard, rigid jointed trees!)
the blinding and red-edged sun-blur—
creeping energy, concentrated
counterforce—welds sky, buds, trees,
rivets them in one puckering hold!
Sticks through! Pulls the whole
counter-pulling mass upward, to the right
locks even the opaque, not yet defined
ground in a terrific drag that is
loosening the very tap-roots!

Just as in Marc's painting we notice in this poem a quality of non-sequential movement—that is, movement which, instead of developing in a linear, "narrative" fashion, moves, circles, as it were, within a narrowly defined visual space.

In one aspect "Spring Strains" is closer to Picasso than

[27] *Ibid.,* 39.

to Marc, for, aside from the "blinding and red-edged sun-blur," which corresponds entirely to Marc's use of the sun in "Tirol," the poem seems to strive consciously for the subdued use of color associated with the analytic phase of Picasso's and Braque's Cubist period. The color scheme of the poem is dominated by a "monotone of blue-grey" and is interrupted only by such closely related colors as "rock blue" and "dirty orange."

Another influence of Cubist painting on the structure of "Spring Strains" finds its origin in the procedure used by the Cubists in visualizing space. Following the example of Cézanne, such painters as Braque, Picasso, and Marc make the space surrounding the objects in their paintings tangible, visible, and active by forcing it into geometric planes. Similarly Williams, in his use of concrete, "visible" words for what are essentially invisible spatial and atmospheric conditions (plastering, puckering, counter-pulling), transfers the visual qualities produced by the materialization of space in painting to verbal equivalents. By using these verbal equivalents in the context of a poem he attains a "Cubist," tactile, visual space in language.

Closely related to the Cubists' practice of materializing space is their tendency to attribute a kind of organic existence to inanimate objects.[28] In Williams this visual tendency is properly assimilated into the realm of language when he makes the trees in a poem such as "Winter Quiet" whirl and "pirouette," or when

> tense with suppressed excitement
> the fences watch where the ground
> has humped an aching shoulder for
>   the ecstasy.

[28] Cf. Kandinsky, *op.cit.*, 36: "Cézanne made a living thing out of a teacup, or rather, in a teacup he realized the existence of something alive. He raised still life to the point where it ceased to be inanimate."

It thus becomes clear that the structure of Williams' poetry, by the time *Al Que Quiere* appeared in 1917, had been drastically influenced by painting. In overall composition as well as in word-choice and selection of visual detail the style of his poems had come to reflect certain developments in the visual arts with an almost uncanny accuracy. This elèment in Williams' poetry distinguished his work from the efforts of his purely literary fellow poets, most of whom were still fettered to the standard rules of Imagism. Few people understood the nature of Williams' innovations, but discerning critics like Conrad Aiken began to see what Williams was trying to do. In a review of *Al Que Quiere* Aiken said: "We get the impression from these poems that [Williams'] world is a world of plane surfaces, bizarrely coloured, and cunningly arranged so as to give an effect of depth and solidity."[29]

Williams' determination to eliminate narrative sequence in his poetry was based, as has been shown, on his desire to achieve the sense of visual unity and, consequently, the immediacy of impression which is associated with painting. The Cubists were said to strive for the further expansion of man's capacity for instantaneous perception by breaking objects into their component parts, and by thus projecting several aspects of these objects, an expanded selection of their structural properties, onto the visual field of a canvas. These

[29] Conrad Aiken, *Scepticisms* (New York 1919), 184. Aiken's comment forms a striking analogy to remarks about Cézanne's theory of composition by Charles Caffin in *Camera Work* (xxxiv-xxxv, April-July 1911). Cézanne argued, Caffin says, "That the painter's designs must be an organized system of planes, composed of objects, plastically real, enveloped in the rhythm of atmospheric depth." These objects "turn upon themselves, and move themselves back; plane passing into plane with an actual movement that is alive."

attempts to intensify the quality of immediate visual experience were based on the concept that a painting exists outside of time or, in Bergson's terms, consists of a point outside the flow of duration. A painting is a spatial structure. Its function is to select, immobilize, and record forms, objects, in nature. As Apollinaire said, "les formes et la matière, violà les objets et les subjets des meilleurs d'entre les peintres d'aujourd'hui."[30] Through his very act of selection and analysis of certain natural forms, the artist could call our attention to the objects themselves, by removing them out of the ever-shifting kaleidoscope of sequential time. Once secured onto the spatial plane of a single canvas, an extensive group of objects would be instantaneously perceptible to the viewer, in a conjunction and interrelationship which would otherwise have remained obscured by the multiplicity of interlocking elements of consciousness in temporal perception. Time, in other words, was a factor dulling the perceptions, and should be thwarted by crowding as much visual experience as possible within the moment of perception represented by the painting. This notion created the concept of Simultaneism in art—now usually associated primarily with Robert Delaunay. In the mid-1910's, however, interest in the possibilities of heightening consciousness, of intensifying our perception, by adding to the furniture of the visual moment of a painting items torn from the normal sequence of experimental time, was widespread. In New York, in the first issue of 291, an anonymous writer (probably Marius de Zayas) defined Simultaneism in painting as "the simultaneous representation of the different figures of a form seen from different points of view, as Picasso or Braque did some time ago; or—the simultaneous representation

[30] Guillaume Apollinaire in Les Soirées de Paris (December 1913), 49.

of the figure of several forms, as the futurists are doing."

To William Carlos Williams the concept of Simultaneism presented a special challenge, with which, considering the direction his poetry was taking, he was bound to have to come to terms. Towards 1917 Williams tried an experiment that was to a certain extent similar to attempts at automatic writing which were having some currency at that time, especially among artists. Every evening he would write down a verbal transcript of the images which his imagination had constructed from the experiences his mind had retained after the exertions of the day. The notations were quick and, once recorded, never changed. Thus he tried to achieve a transposition into the realm of language of the visual structures presented by the imagination in its state of heightened consciousness and intensified perception.

After engaging in this experiment for nearly a year, Williams selected the most effective of his impressionistic notations, and published them, together with the most important of his early essays, as *Kora in Hell; Improvisations* (1920). The "Prologue"[31] contains many admiring references to artists, and a number of rather condescending ones to writers. Williams by this time clearly sought to align his work with that of the painters. "It is to the inventive imagination [that] we look for deliverance," he announced, and he added, "if the inventive imagination must look, as I think, to the field of art for its richest discoveries today, it will best make its way by compass and follow no path." He proposed a "museum of works of spontaneous creation," and emphasized the importance of Duchamp's "Ready-mades" as "compositions," implicitly justifying the seemingly haphazard nature of his own improvisations by repeating

[31] Dated by Williams: "September 1, 1918."

Duchamp's dictum that "a stained-glass window that [has] fallen and [lies] more or less together on the ground [is] of far greater interest than the thing conventionally composed *in situ*." By quoting Kandinsky's *The Spiritual in Art* on the role of the artist, Williams consciously indicated that the subtitle of *Kora in Hell* is a bow to the "Improvisations" of that artist, who in this essay defined these paintings as "a largely unconscious, spontaneous expression of inner character."

In approximating the "spontaneous creation" of the painters, Williams had to come to terms with the problem of time in writing, for he wanted to create a kind of poetic notation that would be analogous to what the painters were doing, "an impressionistic view of the simultaneous." For, as he said in *Kora*, "time is only another liar."

As has already been noted, the Cubists had not been satisfied with the conventional method of representing objects as the eye sees them. They so modulated the elements of visual perception that in looking at their paintings one saw more in an instant than one could experience in an instant of everyday life. Instead of showing only the side of an object turned to the spectator, the Cubists recreated the object in its entirety, trying to give the viewer a more comprehensive, instantaneous understanding of the complex of form that gives a bowl its quality of being a bowl; they tried to present a new, more intense view of reality. Moreover, since a painting represents our perception of an instant of time suspended in the continuous flow of experience,[32] they tried

[32] An early and concise formulation of this concept in art stems from Alfred Jarry, who in a speech presented at the Salon des Indépendents in 1901, said: "La littérature est obligée de faire défiler successivement et un à un les objets qu'elle décrit" mais "dans un tableau le spectateur embrasse d'un coup d'oeil un

to amplify the range of experience covered in an instant of perception by assembling a group of objects, or even by representing a series of events, which in the everyday world would be far beyond our range of instantaneous comprehension. The complex of experience, for instance, in Robert Delaunay's "The Town of Paris" is such that it would usurp a considerable length of time to experience in actual life all the aspects of the real world which are contained in it, while the deteriorating influence inherent in the movement of time would rob the long sequence of perception which it represents of its intensity if it were contained in the actual world (Plate v).

Delaunay, however, by rearranging the usual lines of perception, and by forcing a sequence of events and of the objects which are representative of that sequence, into the instant of time of his painting, has not only prevented the loss of intensity that time forces upon any experience involving such a sequence of events, but has actually intensified our understanding of each object beyond the range of our usual power of perception: He has intensified the complex of reality by rearranging on his canvas the traditional lines of temporal experience, so that the experience becomes instantaneous rather than sequential: "car dans la peinture tout se présente à la fois, l'oeil peut errer sur le tableau, revenir sur telle couleur, regarder d'abord de bas en haut ou faire le contraire, [mais] dans la musique, dans la littérature, tout se succède et l'on ne peut revenir sur tel mot, sur tel son au hasard."[33] In an important sense the very fact

---

aussi grand nombre d'objets, simultanés, qu'il a plu au peintre d'en rassembler." And: "Ainsi donc le tableau ou la statue saisit et fixe un moment de la durée." See Alfred Jarry, "Le Temps dans l'art," *Cahiers du Collège de Pataphysique*, Nouvelle série, Dossier iii, 5-20.

[33] Apollinaire, *op.cit.*

that the eye can roam over a canvas at will ultimately serves to reintegrate the aesthetic experience of viewing a painting into the Bergsonian pattern of intuitive transference of experimental data within duration. For initially the role of a painter such as Delaunay is to introduce order among a number of successive elements, so that their successive quality is converted into the simultaneity created by their projection onto the common spatial field of the canvas. Subsequently, however, the eye of the viewer, roaming over the canvas, perceives the elements, the objects depicted, in multiple random relationships, and hence reintegrates these objects into a succession of interpenetrating visual structures. The act of viewing a painting can therefore be considered as occurring within pure duration.

It should be clear from the foregoing that the notion of simultaneity in painting is due to a propitious case of intellectual fence-straddling by the Futurists, the Cubists, and Apollinaire, who used Bergsonian notions insofar as they could help in explaining and developing the new forms of painting, but who had very little concern for the fact that they were doing violence to the basic concepts of Bergson's philosophy.

Williams did not have any of Apollinaire's doubts about the viability of simultaneity in poetry. He took his cue from the manner in which objects were juxtaposed at will in certain paintings by Delaunay and others, and proceeded to do with language what they were doing with paint. The result was *Kora in Hell*. He did not, like the painters, have the benefit of working within a medium whose products are instantly perceptible. Words follow each other; each occupies its place in time. At the same time, however, writing can represent the thoughts of a person and his reactions to sense impressions. By barraging the reader with a non-logically constructed sequence of direct sense impressions, and by combining the thoughts or the voices of three or four people within a specific instant of time in an inconsequential sequence, the poet will succeed in breaking the impression of the flow of time. Each sentence becomes a separate "object." We thus get what the author of the anonymous note on Simultaneism in 291 calls a "polyphony of simultaneous voices." An instant of time is in this manner endowed with an intensity of experience far beyond the capacity of our usual perception. Logical sequences of images, therefore, such as we find in Williams' earlier poems, are supplanted by a mixture of sounds and images not directly related in time, or for that matter, in space, but caught up, as it were, in their flow and suspended in one clearly delineated field of action. Each section of the Improvisations is such a field of action, in which the reader can read according to whatever sequence he wishes. He can, and is of course likely to, start at the beginning, but nothing is lost if he were to start somewhere in the middle, or at the end, and read the improvisation from the last sentence to the first in reverse order. Or, as Williams himself expressed it in *Kora*: "The stream of things having composed itself into wiry strands that move in one fixed direction, the poet in desperation turns at right angles and cuts across current with startling results to his hangdog mood."[34] Time must be thwarted, so that "the end drives back upon the beginning" (35), for "there is neither beginning nor end to the imagination but it delights in its own seasons, reversing the usual order at will" (37). In *Kora* Williams does reverse the usual order at will, and thus by describing objects and chains of occurrences without regard for logical sequence and in combining

[34] *Kora in Hell; Improvisations* (Boston 1920), 20. Subsequent page references in the text are to this edition.

them to form a panorama of disparate but interlocking events, he robs experience of its temporal quality and brings it as close to immediacy as language can, following in this quite closely the procedure of the painters:

"It is still warm enough to slip from the weeds into the lake's edge, your clothes blushing in the grass and three small boys grinning behind the derelict hearth's side. But summer is up among the huckleberries near the path's end and snakes' eggs lie curling in the sun on the lonely summit. But—well—let's wish it were higher after all these years staring at it deplore the paunched clouds glimpse the sky's thin counter-crest and plunge into the gulch. Sticky cobwebs tell of feverish midnights. Crack a rock (what's a thousand years!) and send it crashing among the oaks! Wind a pine tree in a grey-worm's net and play it for a trout; oh—but it's the moon does that! No, summer has gone down the other side of the mountain. Carry home what we can. What have you brought off? Ah here are thimbleberries." (VII, 1)

A drawing by Stuart Davis was included in the first edition of *Kora in Hell*, showing human figures in the center of a group of scenes and objects representing town, country, home, and the factory—many aspects of a complex of daily experience made instantaneously perceptible and intensified beyond common reality (Plate VI). Later Williams explained in detail why it had been included: "I had seen a drawing by Stuart Davis, a young artist I had never met, which I wanted reproduced in my book because it was as close as possible to my idea of the Improvisations. It was, graphically, exactly what I was trying to do in words, put the Improvisations down as a unit on the page. You must remember I had a strong inclination all my life to be a painter. Under different circumstances I would rather have been a painter than to bother with these god-damn words. I never actually thought of myself as a poet but I knew I had to be an artist in some way. Becoming a poet was the way life arranged it. Anyhow, Floss and I went to Gloucester and got permission from Stuart Davis to use his art—an impressionistic view of the simultaneous."[35]

What Williams tried to do then, in *Kora in Hell*, as he had already tried to do in some of his earlier poems, was to isolate aspects of the visual world, and combine them in such a manner that what was sequential in the world of physical existence became instantaneous in the work of art derived from it. This he achieved through a redistribution of the forms of nature, which, in turn, he effected by rearranging the traditional lines of experience until they accorded with the constructs of his imagination. Thus the reader is presented with a new aspect of reality which intensifies the emotive power of the experience in question, because the sentence and image fragmentation, which in writing inevitably result from such a procedure, approximate far more closely than a conventionally structured piece of writing the constructs of the poet's creative imagination (which, as has been shown, Williams took to be a mental kaleidoscope consisting of old and new images, whole objects, and fragments of last year's as well as yesterday's experiences).[36]

[35] *I Wanted To Write a Poem*, 29.

[36] In the unpublished ms. at Buffalo entitled "What Is The Use of Poetry?" previously referred to, Williams tries to explain the working of the imagination as follows: "Poetry returns authority to man by grace of the imagination. Some intimation of the character of this force may be discovered, I think, in the much greater interest felt in the snatches of pictures shown at the movies between the regular films, to advertise pictures coming the following week, than the regular features themselves. The experience is of something much more vivid and much more

Sentence and image fragmentation, which make a poem into a "canvas of broken parts,"[37] became basic features of Williams' poetry. After experimenting with these techniques in poems such as "Spring Strains" and "March" he made them his basic stylistic concern in *Kora in Hell*, and thus created a literary synthesis of the Cubists' "fragmentary presentation of the image,"[38] of the interplay of forms and colors in Kandinsky, and of the realistic configurations of interacting objects in Stuart Davis' frontispiece. Williams never forgot what he had learned from these sources. Even the structure of *Paterson* is an inevitable result of their influence.

After *Kora in Hell* Williams continued to experiment with the techniques he had learned from the visual arts during the years between 1913 and 1917. Many of the poems in his next book of poetry, *Sour Grapes* (1921), reflect these efforts. "The Great Figure" is perhaps one of the most effective. In his *Autobiography* Williams recalls the circumstances of its genesis: "Once on a hot July day coming back exhausted from the Post Graduate Clinic, I dropped in as I sometimes did at Marsden [Hartley]'s studio on Fifteenth Street for a talk, a little drink maybe and to see what he was doing. As I approached his number I heard a great clatter of bells and the roar of a fire engine passing the end of the street down Ninth Avenue. I turned just in time to see a golden figure 5 on a red background flash by. The impression was so sudden and forceful that I took a piece of paper out of my pocket and wrote a short poem about it."[39]

---

sensual than the entire film will be. It is because the banality of the sequence has been removed."

[37] William Carlos Williams, "The Broken Vase," unpublished ms. in the Yale Library Collection of American Literature.

[38] William Carlos Williams, quoted by John C. Thirlwall, *op.cit.*, 292.

[39] *Autobiography*, 172.

The image "flashes" onto the poet's field of awareness,
is suspended and lifted outside the sequence of time—
a snapshot taken by the poet's perception, as it were—
and when the imagination takes hold of it the action
has been caught and because of that continues forever:

> Among the rain
> and lights
> I saw the figure 5
> in gold
> on a red
> firetruck
> moving
> tense
> unheeded
> to gong clangs
> siren howls
> and wheels rumbling
> through the dark city.

Movement is stilled within time, but continues on a
new, strictly limited, plane outside of time, determined
no longer by actual progression but by visual tensions.
The poet now analyzes the details of his unit of perception and transposes them by means of verbal equivalents
onto paper in the order of their visual importance. The
poem is the painting which results, its words are the
pigment. The effects of instantaneous perception and
of continued movement lifted out of the usual sequence
and development of time which result could not have
been achieved by a prose statement or a conventional
poem dependent on narrative sequence and metaphor,
which would have failed to isolate the incident in its
original intensity. The poem as it stands is the product of
a visual experience and should be regarded as such. If
it is approached from within a literary framework it loses
its significance. Hence when an otherwise perceptive lit-

erary critic such as John Malcolm Brinnin, who in fact
recognizes certain aspects of Williams' indebtedness to
painting, complains that in the case of "The Great
Figure" the poetic version "muddies the simplicity of
the prose statement" in the *Autobiography*, he does so
because he refuses to see the poem in visual rather than
literary terms. This becomes obvious when Brinnin adds
that "the possibility that the figure 5, or any other figure,
on a fire engine might be 'tense' is absurd."[40] One look
at Charles Demuth's visual interpretation of the poem,
executed in close association with Williams,[41] should
suffice to indicate the appropriateness and accuracy of
Williams' use of the word "tense." Demuth's figure 5
strains and pulls, receding and projecting itself again
onto the canvas, its original movement in time transformed into visual tensions, caught within the warring
pressure lines of darkness and lamplight, a golden object
held suspended on the red fires of sound (Plate vii).
Demuth and Williams, men with a similar background
and both profoundly interested in painting and literature, understood each other's creations because their
understanding of the nature of the creative imagination
was similar and because the development of their means
of expression had been determined by the same sources.
The visual power of Williams' original image and
Demuth's transposition of it into what might be called
its "native" visual medium is indeed so strong that it
still has the force to inspire artists of an entirely new
generation.[42]

Williams' fundamental stylistic indebtedness to art,

[40] See John Malcolm Brinnin, *William Carlos Williams* (Minneapolis 1963), 28.

[41] See William Carlos Williams, *Selected Letters*, 97-98.

[42] Robert Indiana's painting "American Dream 1928-1963" is
based on Demuth's "The Great Figure."

and especially to painting after Cézanne, is unmistakable. One cannot explain the development of Williams' poetry exclusively, or even primarily, in terms of Imagism, the influence of Whitman, or Pound. To do so is impossible considering the individual nature of Williams' poetry, and evinces a kind of literary provincialism entirely alien to the artistic temper of a man like Williams. On the other hand, to try to explain Williams' development exclusively in terms of his interest for the visual arts would be equally foolish. Strong influences from both literature and painting exist side by side. Ultimately Williams was a poet, not a painter, even if he regarded his words as paint. Many of his poems do not fall into the stylistic categories discussed here. But even in these poems the techniques Williams learned from the visual arts, once defined, will be seen to have their function. The shock of the Armory Show and the feverish activity of the years that followed created such a wealth of sources for Williams that it is impossible—and unnecessary—to try to determine precisely which artists or which paintings were originally decisive. Certain influences, those of Cézanne, Matisse, Picasso, and Duchamp, as well as, later on in the Twenties, Juan Gris and the Surrealists, were inevitable. But the greatest influence was the combined impact of these artists and their followers.

As the 1910's drew to a close, however, a conflict between the basic concerns of Williams' poetry and the direction European art was taking became evident. Beginning with *Sour Grapes* many of Williams' poems cease to focus on the fragmentation or destruction of objects. Instead they would seem to reflect what Max Goth in 1917, in one of the issues of 391, derides as a sign of feeblemindedness in a modern artist: "Trois pommes sur un compotier, nous l'avons dit, peuvent

79

induire tel fils d'Adam en un perpétuel étonnement. Trois pommes sont trois pommes. Et c'est vert. Et c'est rouge. Et c'est rond. Ces découvertes peuvent suffire à toute une vie." Artists who are satisfied with this kind of thing do not have any "faculté d'invention" according to Goth.[43]

Clearly a disparity was beginning to show itself between Williams' poetic interests and the radical steps being taken by the European artists toward abstraction or toward the more destructive aspects of Dadaism. Williams continued to appreciate their work and to draw from it but the focus of his allegiance was shifting. He had only recently discovered the object as artistic unit and it appeared to him, as well as to a number of the American painters who had found their inspiration in the new European art movements represented in the Armory Show, that to indulge in the wholesale destruction of their new discovery would represent a prodigal squandering of pictorial resources. The Americans, therefore, while retaining to a large extent the techniques learned from the French, returned to representational forms and began to concentrate on the analysis and careful construction of objects. They began to use their newly discovered methods of visual notation to explore and define the content of the American scene. In this their mentor was Alfred Stieglitz, who had provided them with a gallery to show their work, when no one else was interested, and who now urged them to be "American." Williams' close friends Charles Demuth and Marsden Hartley were central figures in the 291 group. Other Stieglitz associates were among the artists Williams most admired. Stieglitz himself, in his photographs, was showing the way to the distinctly "American" object. Thus when Williams began to look for a way in which to

[43] Picabia, 391, 30.

express his sense of the American experience, he found himself irresistibly drawn to the methods and concepts of the painters and writers who had grouped themselves in a very casual fashion around the socratic figure of Stieglitz.

III. STIEGLITZ

*t*HERE is a close connection between many features of Williams' theory concerning the responsibilities of the artist toward the world of concrete perception, and the concepts developed by Alfred Stieglitz and his associates. There are also striking similarities between many of Williams' poems and the paintings of such artists as John Marin, Marsden Hartley, and Arthur Dove. Some of Stieglitz's photographs reappear in Williams' work, translated into language. Yet the relationship between the poet and the Stieglitz circle has been largely ignored. For this omission Williams himself must certainly bear the primary responsibility. He was a volatile, impulsive man, and, in the heat of his assertions, rarely concerned with their accuracy. He did not like to be pinned down to any specific position or group; especially in discussing his poetry, he was wary not to be too explicit about his sources of influence. The *Autobiography* (1951) represents this aspect of Williams' character quite fully, the more because it did not benefit from his wife's tempering influence. Florence Williams usually read her husband's writings before they were published, suggesting changes which might improve their factual accuracy. But in a fit of independence Williams had insisted that she forego her role as editor in the case of the *Autobiography*. Perhaps he realized that she would not have condoned his fanciful elaborations, as well as his omissions. In any case, Mrs. Williams did not see the manuscript before its publication. Later she remarked: "I wish I had, there were so many errors in the *Autobiography*. That was inexcusable."[1] Yet in most cases it is on this

[1] Stanley Koehler, "The Art of Poetry, An Interview with William Carlos Williams," *The Paris Review*, 32 (Summer-Fall 1964), 111-151.

work that Williams' critics have to depend for their factual information about Williams' life and his attitude towards his acquaintances.

Writing his autobiography must have been in many ways a purgative process for Williams. During the 1940's he seems to have come very close to a general breakdown of spirit. He was especially sensitive to what he considered the nearly willful neglect of his poetry by the public and his continued dependence on little magazines to get his work published. His ability to judge fairly had been taxed by the contradictory demands which patriotism and friendship placed upon him in such matters as the wartime behavior and subsequent public persecution of Ezra Pound. He was always willing to be reckless, and in his agitation he wrote a rather puerile *ad hominem* denunciation of Pound, titled "E. 'Lackwit' Pound," which mercifully remained unpublished.[2] In the *Autobiography*, however, Williams portrays himself as a loyal, tolerant friend to Pound in the difficult years following the war.

When Stieglitz died in 1946, Dorothy Norman asked Williams to contribute to a memorial volume. The poet sent her a manuscript which was as intemperate as his piece on Pound. Almost incredibly, so immediately after the horrors of nazi Germany, the piece had sharp overtones of anti-Semitism. Like so many of his liberal, intellectual friends, Williams resorted to racial innuendo when he was overwrought—although, of course, some of his best friends were Jews.[3] According to Mrs. Norman,

[2] It is to be found in the Williams mss. Collection of the Lockwood Memorial Library of the State University of New York at Buffalo.

[3] For some unpleasant insights into this particular aspect of Williams' character see his semi-autobiographical novel, *A Voyage to Pagany* (New York 1928), especially pp. 174, 176, and 178, where we are presented with some Jewish stereotypes which anticipate the loaded characterization of the literature of the Third Reich. On page 285 one can find the following sentence:

Williams' vehement reaction was due to an unfortunate episode with Stieglitz which took place at some time during the last years of Stieglitz's life, and which involved a painting by John Marin. The incident itself can be seen as indicative of the instability of Williams' judgment at the time. Williams, apparently, had taken a great liking to a certain work by Marin in Stieglitz's gallery, "An American Place." He wanted to buy it but insisted that Stieglitz allow him a special price since they were old friends. As Williams must have known very well, this was asking Stieglitz to compromise what he considered a sacred trust as Marin's protector against the machinations of the business world, and of course Stieglitz refused to bargain. In the heat of his disappointment Williams' assumption seems to have been that Stieglitz was only keeping the price high because this would bring him a larger commission. Had Williams stopped to reflect he would have recognized the unfairness of that assumption, for it was common knowledge that Stieglitz did not run his gallery as a business and received no monetary compensation for his efforts in selling the canvases he had been entrusted with by the artists who were his protégés. The manuscript of Williams' "memorial" to Stieglitz would seem to corroborate Mrs. Norman's account of the altercation, for it contains several otherwise inexplicable allusions to the photographer's supposedly rather mercenary nature.

The episode may explain partly why Williams paid so little attention to Stieglitz in his *Autobiography*, and why, when he did come to talk about him, he attempted to intimate that his acquaintance with Stieglitz had been on the whole an unimportant one. At times, indeed,

"A Jew of the usual objectional type made himself objectionable by closing the door to the compartment and smoking copiously, a vile smell. . . ."

Williams engaged in deliberate misrepresentation of fact to cover up his connection with the photographer. He tried to suggest, in effect, that he had come to know Stieglitz as a result of the publication of *In the American Grain* (1925): "As a book it fell flat," he said. "However I made some friends. Stieglitz found the book somewhere and wrote enthusiastically to me about it. He even said it had given him the name, An American Place, when he moved to the new site for his gallery on Madison Avenue. From that time forward for many years, until Stieglitz's somewhat crotchety old age I frequented that gallery. But when he dropped Hartley I began to fall off from him. He talked me deaf dumb and blind. I tremendously admired him, as I did Georgia O'Keeffe, his wife, but I couldn't take it any more. Later I took a small part in Dorothy Norman's enterprise, *Twice A Year*, but it was too much for me, my direction had shifted."[4]

Williams' claim that he "fell off" from Stieglitz "when he dropped Hartley" rings especially false. Sticglitz never "dropped" Hartley, although there were some quarrels of a minor nature between the two from time to time throughout their acquaintance. In Williams' *Selected Letters*, moreover, there is a long note from the poet to Stieglitz discussing the possibilities of his editorial participation in the projected magazine *Twice a Year*. The letter ends with a detailed appreciation of Marsden Hartley's current show at An American Place.[5] This was in 1937, only a few years before Hartley's death. The gallery which Stieglitz opened in 1925 was not called "An American Place," but "The Intimate Gallery." An American Place came into existence only in 1929, when Stieglitz moved his gallery to a different location. This

[4] Williams, *Autobiography*, 236.
[5] *Selected Letters*, 166-68.

latter inaccuracy may reasonably be ascribed to Williams' shaky memory, but his intimation that Stieglitz became an acquaintance of his only after *In the American Grain* was published cannot be seen as anything but conscious misrepresentation. For Williams had already been on very friendly terms with Stieglitz for a number of years before this book appeared. The years before its appearance were in fact notable for Williams' close association with the Stieglitz group. A letter by Williams to Stieglitz, dated January 12, 1922, preserved in the Stieglitz Archive at Yale University, presents incontrovertible evidence that by this time they knew each other quite intimately. Stieglitz had sent Williams a copy of Marsden Hartley's book of essays, *Adventures in the Arts*, which had just been published by Boni and Liveright, largely at Stieglitz's instigation. Williams wrote back to thank him, and remarked that he would "stop in to see you at your rooms some evening soon, perhaps tomorrow. Do not alter any of your plans on my account but unless something unforeseen occurs (I am a slave you know) I shall appear at your place this Friday evening at perhaps eight o'clock." Williams closed his letter by remarking: "it has been a nice quiet winter hasn't it with everybody away."—a statement which presupposes the existence of common acquaintances and shared experiences. It seems, in fact, highly unlikely that Williams would have been able to avoid running into Stieglitz early during the 1910's. The central importance of the figure of the photographer in the small avant garde circle of New York at that time has already been discussed. Williams' closest friends of those years, Charles Demuth and Alfred Kreymborg, were among the most faithful champions of Stieglitz and his gallery 291, and nearly everyone else among the artists Williams knew during that period, from Marsden Hartley to Marianne Moore, had some connection with the man or the place.

There is a good reason why Williams would have wished to muffle the facts of his close connection with Stieglitz and the Stieglitz circle. In many of his writings, in his poetry as well as in his prose, Williams betrays a special sensitivity to the belief apparently current among his acquaintances or perhaps merely present primarily in his own mind that he was not much of a thinker or theorist. It may have seemed to him that to admit the influence of Stieglitz's theories would have threatened his claim to originality, and, as has been pointed out, the notion of originality, to have new ideas, to "make it new," was central to his concept of the role of the artist.

Had Stieglitz lived long enough to witness Williams' concerted effort to obscure the facts of their long acquaintance, the spectacle would not have surprised him. Throughout Stieglitz's life one of his main principles had been not to compromise the integrity of his artistic and personal standards. To many people who had been, or had wanted to be, close to him at various stages of his career, and who conceived of friendship as being above integrity, the rigidity of his demands for excellence in his associates as well as in himself were exasperating. They accused him of insincerity, pomposity, and a grossly exaggerated estimate of his own importance. It was nearly impossible to remain neutral about the figure of Stieglitz. To most of his followers he was indeed a socratic presence. His strength of character and his self-assurance gave him an almost mythic stature to many. To those whom he offended by negative judgments on their creative efforts he became like an ogre, a living representation of their doubts about themselves. As a result Stieglitz had nearly as many virulent enemies as devoted followers;

many of those enemies had, at one time or another, been his friends. Williams' final rejection of Stieglitz may very well have something to do with the fact that Stieglitz, throughout their acquaintance, maintained serious doubts about the value of Williams' poetry.

Stieglitz's parents had been German immigrants, but he was quite emphatic about the nature of his cultural framework. "I was born in Hoboken," he used to say, "I am an American." These two facts were of supreme importance to him, and from his earliest ventures into the world of art he attempted to cope with their implications. During the 1880's as a student at the Berlin Polytechnic Institute, where he had been sent by his parents to study mechanical engineering, he faithfully defended his country against attacks by Europeans who regarded America with cynical detachment as an amorphous, colossal, and sub-literate monstrosity. An early fascination with the new science of the camera led him to abandon engineering in 1883, but he remained at the university in Berlin to obtain a thorough knowledge of the scientific aspects of photography. He soon earned a considerable reputation for his work in Europe.

When Stieglitz returned to the United States in 1890, he quickly became a leader among American photographers, always insisting on the dignity of photography as a means of creative expression and emphasizing the propriety of regarding its best products as genuine works of art. But homecoming held an unpleasant shock for him. The "glowing vision of America" and its promise which had animated him in Europe, disappeared. "Once back in New York, I experienced an intense longing for Europe; for its vital tradition of music, theatre, art and craftsmanship." He felt only revulsion against the hard, gargantuan, industrial world around him. Then, after an extraordinary performance by Eleanora Duse in *Camille*, he began to regain faith in the possibilities of America. "I felt, for the first time since I had left Europe, that there was a contact between myself and my country once more."[6] If the New World could present and appreciate international artists of Duse's talent, then there was yet hope for its survival. He began to rediscover America in his own way, with his camera. The rural beauties of Europe had fascinated him until now: the mountains, the tree-lined roads, the picturesque street passages of Venice and the clusters of children playing, the equally picturesque Venetian beggar boy in his rags. But these photographs, although remarkably evocative, fitted closely with the public concept of "Art" at the time: they were romantic, "pretty," anecdotal. Yet, in 1887, when he photographed the Venetian boy, an unorthodox element had crept into his treatment of the subject: the camera had come uncomfortably close to the boy. His blond curls, which should have been so pretty, had turned out to be dirty; his clothes were not picturesque tatters— they were real, sadly real, rags. The boy's face, too, was too sharply focused for comfort: the handsome young features were marred by the scars, creases, and puffed eyelids of a worn-out old man. The result was not the sort of thing to find approval in the Salons.

In 1892 Stieglitz's desire to reestablish his lost "contact" with America drove him out onto the streets of Manhattan. He photographed trolley-car horses, steaming, worn out in the snow, being watered at the line terminal by a weary, freezing attendant. "There seemed to be something closely related to my deepest feeling in what I saw, and I decided to photograph what was with-

[6] Quoted in Dorothy Norman, *Alfred Stieglitz, Portrait of an American Seer* (New York 1960), 9.

in me," Stieglitz said.[7] He went out into a snowstorm and photographed a horse-drawn coach as it was lumbering heavily against the flailing winds. The picture, "Winter-Fifth Avenue," was a technical feat, considered impossible at the time, but it was also a remarkable composition: the coach forcing itself forward out of a vortex of converging lines of trees, sidewalks, buildings and cartwheel tracks, into the driving snow. The picture was sharply focused, notwithstanding the blurring effect of the storm.

In subjects such as these Stieglitz explored what he considered to be the essence of America. At the same time he became, almost in passing, one of the important innovators of camera technique. His unusual subject matter and his opinionated pronouncements on style made him a center of controversy among photographers. He was a flamboyant man with a great sense of drama, a strong belief in his own genius, and an overwhelming sense of mission: he saw the potential of America as a source of important indigenous art, but he also saw how those in America who might have created an American art were completely dependent upon Europe for their inspiration. In photography this dependence was apparent in the attempts of nearly all photographers to obtain hazy, "impressionistic" pictures whenever they meant to be "serious." To this end they scratched their plates or tried to soften outlines by giving the negatives a special treatment designed to make the prints look smoky. The photographs invariably seemed taken in fog, vague landscapes blurring the backgrounds, while somewhere between leaves or dusky trees a wispy female figure in long robes might float about, or, at best, stand, holding a large glass bowl which, more often than not, would

[7] *Ibid.*

look like a colossal soap bubble. Often the photographer would pose a plump ballerina in some impossible position, pin her veils in various "floating" positions against the curtain behind her, and hope, on taking her picture after all this, to be able to catch "the spontaneous grace of the dance." Special papers were used to make it seem as if the prints were on canvas. The photographers, in other words, aimed for a painterly effect, and hunted for landscapes or subjects which, when turned into photographs, would look just like paintings. Most of them suffered from a great sense of inferiority. No one assumed that "Art" could be created with "a machine"—the camera was an industrial product and photography seemed a child of the assembly line. In a desperate attempt to gain legitimate standing as artists, the photographers—in Europe as well as the United States—followed the lead of the painters in selecting their subjects, and in their manner of presentation. "Pretty" pictures were the order of the day.

Thus when in the mid 1890's Stieglitz went out into the snow to photograph work horses and workmen and muddy streets, or to catch carriages waiting in a black rainy night before an expensive restaurant blazing with light, he was breaking convention as well as performing technical feats. Always closely interested in the newest forms of expression in the visual arts, he showed in these pictures that he understood the reasons for the Impressionists' preoccupation with the modulating power of light. But he also accepted the fact that a camera would never be capable of producing the diffusion of color particles which gave Impressionist paintings their singular merit. He knew that the primary quality of photography was its ability to record elements of the visual world with a sharpness of outline and accuracy of detail unattainable to the painter. He therefore discarded all attempts to imitate painting and focused his pictures carefully, rejoicing in the needle-sharp clarity of his prints. As Marianne Moore has said, he "had no gift for subterfuge . . . , his horses in a blizzard did not have to be zebras."[8] A famous photograph of 1902, "The Hand of Man," shows a lonely locomotive on a grim, soggy winter day, laboring forward out of an empty trainyard, spitting a column of filthy smoke into the air. Stieglitz made no effort to blur the ugly disorder of the railway yard, the telephone poles and wires, dirt on the ground, smokestacks and factories in the distance. The locomotive is sluggish, but capable of speed on the sharp, cold, polished steel of the tracks. The photograph is striking in its cold severity, in the sense of desolation it conveys, and in its structural simplicity (Plate viii).

Photographs such as this, using sharp contrasts of black and white, using the true possibilities of photography, were to become the trademark of Stieglitz's technique. His discovery of the "unpoetic" aspects of New York antedates the work of the Ashcan School in painting. The Eight, in fact, joined forces with Stieglitz's Photo Secession group in January 1908 during an exhibition at the National Arts Club. The painters of the Ashcan group knew Stieglitz and had seen his work. It is by no means impossible that their movement gained some ideas from this acquaintance. Among champions of Stieglitz's cause, indeed, claims were current that the photographer's work had been an important influence on the development of their concepts about the function of art. Stieglitz's prints, and especially "Winter-Fifth Avenue," it was said, "created a sensation not only in photographic circles, but in

[8] Marianne Moore in *Stieglitz Memorial Portfolio: Tributes In Memoriam*, compiled by Dorothy Norman (New York 1947).

the world of art, and blazed the way for a whole school of painters who set themselves the task of depicting the streets and life of New York."[9] It is understandable that comments of this nature created a great deal of animosity against Stieglitz among the Eight, and their reminiscences of Stieglitz tend to be unfriendly. Yet Stieglitz's photographs did strike many people as "sensational." Theodore Dreiser, who around the turn of the century wrote no less than three articles on Stieglitz, saw in them authentic records of city life, and when he came to write his portrait of a painter, *The Genius*, his descriptions of Eugene Witla's paintings often resemble photographs by Stieglitz more nearly than the work of the Eight.[10]

City realism was an innovation which exhausted the desire for revolution of such painters as Luks, Glackens, and Sloan. The subsequent developments in the art world destroyed their position as rebels almost as soon as they had gained it, and eclipsed their achievement. But Stieglitz's explorations of the "ugly" city were but means to an end, pictures "of the New America that was still in the making."[11] He saw the new art of Paris as a tool with which he could, paradoxically, pry American art loose from its dependence on Europe. As part of that process he could then establish the independence of photography as an art. In opening 291 to the avant garde he deliberately emphasized both the differences and the underlying similarities between painting and photography. He was hopeful from the first that the work of Cézanne, Matisse, Picasso, and Kandinsky, juxtaposed with his own photography, might be instrumental in creating an

[9] J. Nilsen Laurvik, "Alfred Stieglitz, Pictorial Photographer," *International Studio*, XLIV, 174 (August 1911), 21-27.

[10] F. O. Mathiessen, in his *Theodore Dreiser* (New York 1951), briefly discussed Dreiser's relationship with Stieglitz.

[11] Quoted in Norman, *Stieglitz*, 16.

atmosphere in New York which would make an American art possible: "America without that damned French flavor," as he wrote to Paul Rosenfeld in 1923.[12] To a correspondent who hoped to exhibit at 291 and who complained that the gallery seemed to have abandoned the cause of photography, he wrote: "The Little Gallery is not devoted entirely to the ultra modern in painting and sculpture. It is devoted to ideas. To the development of such. And I feel that your work, good as it is, is primarily picture making. That it is not adding anything to the idea of photography, nor to the idea of expression. And for that reason it would be out of place in the Little Gallery."[13]

All Stieglitz's activities from the opening of the "Little Gallery" in 1905 onward, and especially throughout the decade between 1910 and 1920, were centered on his search for an art which would express itself in terms of its native context: "I had been thinking of America constantly in the days before the war. What was 291 but a thinking of America?"[14] Stieglitz liked to say that 291 was representative of something much larger than himself, that its significance was determined by the collective interests of the artists and writers who gathered there. In an important sense this is true. Stieglitz never insisted that the artists associated with him follow a narrowly circumscribed style. But at the same time he knew very well what he was looking for. All he did as a photographer, as editor, as gallery owner, as friend, was part of an elaborate process of selection and synthesis. As such

[12] Unpublished letter, September 5, 1923, Stieglitz Archive, Yale.

[13] Unpublished letter to "Miss Parish," May 8, 1917, Stieglitz Archive, Yale.

[14] Alfred Stieglitz, "Ten Stories," *Twice a Year*, v-vi (1940-1941), 135-63.

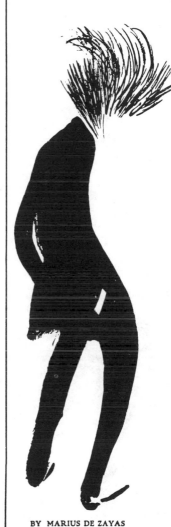

Camera Work

THE MAGAZINE WITH-
OUT AN "IF"—FEARLESS—
INDEPENDENT—WITH-
OUT FAVOR ☐   ☐   ☐

BY MARIUS DE ZAYAS

1. Marius de Zayas, Alfred Stieglitz and *Camera Work*
(reprinted from *Camera Work*, Nr. XXX, April 1910).

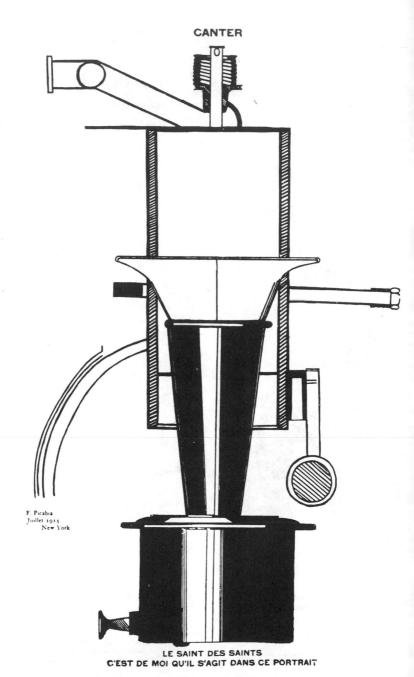

CANTER

F. Picabia
Juillet 1915
New York

LE SAINT DES SAINTS
C'EST DE MOI QU'IL S'AGIT DANS CE PORTRAIT

II. Francis Picabia, A Page from *291*
(reprinted from *291*, Nr. 5-6, July-August 1915).

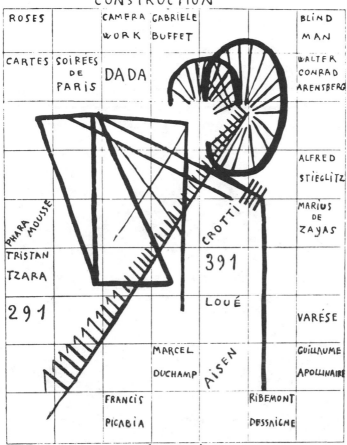

III. Francis Picabia, A Page from *391*
(reprinted from *391*, Nr. 8, February 1919).

IV. Franz Marc, Tirol, 1912-1914
(Neue Staatsgalerie, Munich).

V. Robert Delaunay, The Town of Paris, 1910-1912
(Musée d'Art Moderne, Paris)

VI. Stuart Davis, Frontispiece to *Kora in Hell*, 1916
(Courtesy Mrs. Stuart Davis).

VII. Charles Demuth, I Saw the Figure 5 in Gold, 1928
(Metropolitan Museum of Art, the Alfred Stieglitz Collection).

VIII. Alfred Stieglitz, The Hand of Man, 1902.

IX. Alfred Stieglitz, Spring Showers, 1902.

X. Alfred Stieglitz, Apples and Gable, Lake George, 1922
(Collection George Eastman House, Rochester)

XI. Alfred Stieglitz, From the Window—"291" (I), 1915
(Museum Fine Arts, Boston)

XII. Alfred Stieglitz, Dancing Trees, 1921.

XIII. Alfred Stieglitz, Clouds in 10 Movements—II, 1921
(Courtesy Miss Doris Bry)

XIV. Arthur Dove, A Walk Poplars, 1920
(Courtesy Mrs. Edith Gregor Halpert, Downtown Gallery).

XV. Arthur Dove, Long Island (Collage), 1925
(Museum of Fine Arts, Boston).

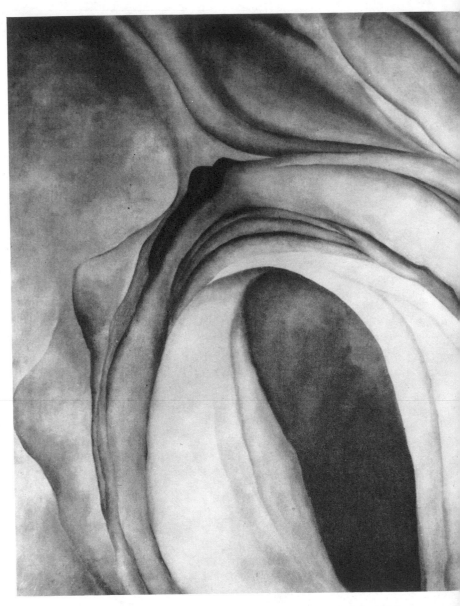

XVI. Georgia O'Keeffe, Music, Pink and Blue, Number 2, 1919 (Collection of the Artist).

XVII. Charles Sheeler, Bucks County Barns, 1923
(Collection of the Whitney Museum of American Art, New York)

XVIII. Charles Sheeler, Classic Landscape, 1931
(Collection Mrs. Edsel B. Ford).

XIX. Charles Demuth, Machinery, 1920
(Metropolitan Museum of Art, the Alfred Stieglitz Collection).

XX. Charles Demuth, Tuberoses, 1922
(Collection Mrs. William Carlos Williams)

XXI. Juan Gris, Roses (Collage), 1914
(Private Collection, Paris).

291 was most certainly Stieglitz. His photographs, first
of all, showed the way, for he continued to explore the
possibilities of the camera, and not until 1937 did he
cease to express himself through it. As director of his
gallery he selected the exhibits very carefully, not only
for their significance as art, but also for their usefulness
as "texts." As editor of *Camera Work*, he chose only
those articles and illustrations which he considered most
representative of the concepts which should underlie the
development of an indigenous American art. Thus while
to the public Stieglitz might seem to be merely an active
member of a heterogeneous group of artists, in private
he was constantly at work to supervise the direction his
artists would take. Moreover, he did not hesitate to
excommunicate those among his associates who had
developed theories inimical to his aims. Early in 1915,
for instance, he told Benjamin de Casseres, whose theories about art were becoming increasingly anarchic: "You
have lost touch with what is really going on at '291'
and in *Camera Work*." This was in response to a manuscript on Odilon Redon which de Casseres had sent him.
Moreover, Stieglitz continued, "I have some of your
MSS still on hand unused. I know I shall never be able
to use them, as they don't fit into what I am doing, or
trying to do."[15]

The kind of approach to art Stieglitz developed in his
photographs, and helped to foster in the artists associated
with him, was based on his belief in sharply focused
photography. As has been already pointed out, he recognized from the very first that the camera's primary merit
was that it was capable of reproducing reality with absolute fidelity. But because the camera will record all things
without discrimination, it is in itself no more a source

[15] Unpublished letter to de Casseres, January 21, 1915, Stieglitz Archive, Yale.

of art than is paint. A painter can use his materials very much in whatever way he wants; the creative process to which he is committed is not limited in time or space: if he so wishes he can spend years on a single painting. He can therefore afford to analyze his subject while he is painting. But an unretouched photograph is the record of a moment, its image is fixed in an instant of time. Stieglitz therefore argued that it is the photographer's role to seize the moment in terms of its most opportune structure. He must select the single image which will represent the object under his scrutiny most effectively. The photographer, therefore, more than any other artist, must be perfectly alert to the materials of the visible world. He is entirely dependent on what exists to the eye; he must see, before he can create. He must, before all, in the most literal sense of the word, be a seer. Stieglitz probably became aware of these implications of photography when he began to use the "snapshot" camera with which he took his earliest pictures of New York. This discovery influenced his approach to the world in an absolute sense, creating the laws on which his further artistic life was based: "The moment dictates for me what I must do," he said. "I have no theory about what the moment should bring. . . . I simply react to the moment. . . . I am the moment."[16] The materials of the "living moment" are the things *seen*. "Beauty is the universal seen," he emphasized, and "in one's way of seeing lies one's way of action."[17] The basis for all that is meaningful in life is man's capacity to see the objective world. "I detest," Stieglitz said, "superstitions that go against life, against truth, against the reality of experience, against the spontaneous living out of the sense of wonder —of fresh experience, freshly seen and communicated."[18]

[16] Quoted in Norman, *op.cit.*, 54.
[17] *Ibid.*   [18] *Ibid.*, 25.

Very early Stieglitz discovered that a photographer must not only be capable of seeing sharply and precisely in order to capture the living moment, but must be unusually selective as well. A photograph representing a complex scene can be effective, but most often the larger the number of objects depicted, the more diffuse the impact of the picture. Hence Stieglitz progressively reduced the visual field presented by his photographs. As early as 1901 Charles Caffin could remark that Stieglitz in his "mature work" invariably emphasized "the important facts of the scene, eliminating or moderating the less important, and bringing every detail into due subordination to a single effect of telling simplicity."[19] Much later Edward Weston was to say that Stieglitz always searched for a way to express "a maximum of detail with a maximum of simplification."[20] Inevitably, as the number of objects in his pictures decreased, the objects which remained received more emphasis. The object within the visible world became the focal point for Stieglitz's art. Within the object the artist finds all he needs to express himself: "There is nothing in my pictures that isn't there—that doesn't come straight from the object photographed."[21] As Paul Strand has said, in Stieglitz's work "every object, every blade of grass, is felt and accounted for."[22]

In the work of Cézanne, Matisse, and the Cubists, Stieglitz found unexpected allies for his views. His photography and the new painting represented two opposite

[19] Charles H. Caffin, "Photography as a Fine Art: The Work of Alfred Stieglitz," *Everybody's Magazine*, IV, 20 (April 1901), 369.

[20] *Stieglitz Memorial Portfolio*, 25.

[21] Quoted in Clarence I. Freed, "Alfred Stieglitz," *The American Hebrew* (January 18, 1924), 305.

[22] Paul Strand, "The Art Motive in Photography," *British Journal of Photography* (October 5, 1923), 612-15.

ways of approaching the objective world. In *Camera Work* article after article emphasized that in the new painting "the age of reality-perception is most clearly exemplified," that, in spite of its tendency towards abstraction it was "not intended as a denial of matter" but on the contrary an affirmation of its importance.[23] The modern painters, it was said, carefully analyzed each object in nature as potentially representative of the full scope of their inner experience. It is in this aspect of their work that Stieglitz saw a significant connection with his own. In a newspaper article introducing the Armory Show, he wrote: "This is what you'll see at the Sixty-ninth Regiment Armory exhibition: all sorts of individual efforts to express with colors and forms individual conceptions of the whole meaning of natural objects." Picabia's "arrangement of color masses" should ultimately be regarded as "a lifelike representation of a living and moving reality."[24] And in *Camera Work*, that same year, Marius de Zayas made the connection explicit. "Stieglitz," he said, "has begun with the elimination of the subject in represented Form to search for the pure expression of the object. He is trying to do synthetically, with the means of a mechanical process, what some of the most advanced artists of the modern movement are trying to do analytically with the means of art."[25] Two years later, in an issue of the magazine 291 which featured a large reproduction of Stieglitz's photograph "The Steerage," de Zayas emphasized the photographer's role "in determining the objectivity of Form": "The desire

[23] John Weichsel, "Cosmism or Amorphism," *Camera Work*, 42-43 (April-July 1913), 69-82.

[24] Alfred Stieglitz, "The First Great Clinic to Revitalize Art," *New York American* (Sunday, January 26, 1913), 5-ce.

[25] Marius de Zayas, "Photography and Artistic Photography," *Camera Work*, 42-43 (April-July 1913), 13-14.

of modern plastic expression has been to create for itself an objectivity. The task accomplished by Stieglitz's photography has been to make objectivity understood, for it has given it the true importance of a natural fact. . . . Stieglitz, in America, through photography, has shown us, as far as it is possible, the objectivity of the outer world."[26]

Stieglitz's discovery of the importance of the object in the real world goes back to the 1890's, to the time when he had begun to reestablish a contact between himself and his country by exploring the realities of New York City. He discovered that in observing carefully the ugly rows of houses, the muddy streets, and the towering skyscrapers, which presumably were merely the outward aspects of American life, he would, at unexpected moments, in unexpected places, see objects or incidents to which his feelings could respond deeply. He discovered why he was American by seeing his emotions paralleled in the objective world of the city around him. Stieglitz always emphasized how alone he had felt in those early years. In the concrete materials of New York he found the objective equivalents to his loneliness: the stiff figure of a man tending car horses; the locomotive in a deserted railroad yard; the *Mauretania* moving silently into harbor; the dirigible moving darkly through a radiant, but empty and cold sky; even the Flat Iron building, a hard, towering silhouette among trees, isolated from the city by a snowstorm. Perhaps the most impressive of these early photographs is the one called "Spring Showers." It shows an empty, wet expanse of sidewalk and street, gritty and shining with pebbles, sand, and rain. A young tree breaks out of the flat, stone surface, its thin trunk scattering into a microscopic tracery of branches and a spotted rhythm of cocoons. Next

[26] Nr. 7-8 (September-October 1915), 1.

to it is an old, bent man, with a huge broom, sweeping the gutter. In the distance are the towering buildings of the city, nearly obliterated by the rain. But at the horizon, a massive line-up of carriages and cars hovers ominously, threatening to shatter in an instant the silence of the man and his tree (Plate IX).

Stieglitz realized through the achievement of these photographs, and through his continuing and ever more precise observation of the objects of concrete reality, that he could express his most intense and therefore most inarticulate emotions accurately in terms of the materials of life. In the lines and textures and shapes of things he found the emotive qualities which, if selected and recorded carefully and precisely, would make the resultant photograph representative of his feelings. But this was not a process detrimental to the reality of the object so used. The object did not become a means to an end. It remained autonomous; the photographer, by focusing on the object in his special way, clarified certain of its hitherto unrecognized but nonetheless inherent qualities which, when understood, would enhance the object's independent significance. Thus the artist could do justice to the object without forcing it to function as a metaphor for something else. The photographer must therefore begin by seeing all things with perfect precision, perfect penetration. If he does so, and if he is closely attuned to the elements of his own subjective experience, he will be able to recognize in certain natural objects around him elements hitherto not yet discovered, but nonetheless eternally present in them, manifested through their shapes, lines, and volumes, which constitute not only equivalences to his original emotions, but are, indeed, factors of the material origins of these emotions. Hence the objects of nature are recognized to be the sources of our spiritual constitution; the content of our non-rational being as much as of our intellectual existence is shown to be determined by the contents of the physical world. Spirit, in other words, derives from matter. The photographer, seeing accurately, discovers in what elements of matter spirit has its origin, and in his photograph, which represents the moment of his discovery, he records the encounter, making his discovery permanently accessible to everyone who is willing to meet the object recorded on its own terms. In this sense the photographer's record of the object is intended to evoke in the observer a kind of Platonic recognition. But in Plato the objects of the natural world are merely shadows of absolutes, means to an end. For Stieglitz the objects of nature are the absolutes from which all derives.

If this is the case, then life finds its most complete fulfillment in the accurate observation of matter: what is seen, felt, and therefore experienced, determines the meaning of life. If all values derive from matter, beauty, for one thing, *must* be the universal *seen*. Often the conventional way of seeing an object, which makes it a "subject" to be scrutinized in relationship to its practical "purpose," rather than a *ding an sich*, obstructs the viewer's perception of the independent meaning of the shapes, lines, and volumes of experience inherent in the object. Stieglitz therefore attempted to abstract the essence of the object as "independent thing" from its obscurantist role as "thing with a use," by photographing ever smaller details: hands, breasts, part of a tree trunk, a doorway, an apple on a bough (Plate x). Ultimately this led him to his famous photographs of clouds:

"I have found that the use of clouds as subject-matter in my photographs has made people less aware of clouds *as clouds* in the pictures, than when I have used trees or houses or wood—or any other objects. In looking at the photographs of clouds, people seem to feel freed to

101

think more about the actual relationships in the pictures and less about the subject-matter as such, so that what I have been trying to say through my photographs seems most clearly communicated in the series of *Songs of the Sky*, where the true meaning of the *Equivalents*, as I have called these photographs, (in reality all my photographs are *Equivalents*), comes through directly, without any extraneous or distracting pictorial or representational factors coming between the person and the picture."[27] In his cloud pictures, in other words, Stieglitz succeeded most completely in eliminating "the subject in represented Form," in order to emphasize "the pure expression of the object." But this did not mean that Stieglitz therefore had abandoned objective reality in order to represent a spiritual structure which found its origin beyond material things. He continued to stress that all he did found its origin and purpose in the world of objects: "The quality of *touch* in its deepest living sense is inherent in my photographs. When that sense of *touch* is lost, the heartbeat of the photograph is extinct."[28] Life, ultimately, finds its meaning within its material self, and because of that it can be meaningful: spirit finds its origin and expression in things, therefore "the feeling, or the desire, that does not generate the moment of action is but mental and not real."[29] But if you take care to permit yourself "to be free to recognize the living moment when it occurs, and to let it flower, without preconceived ideas about what it *should* be," then you *are* the moment.[30] "When I am no longer thinking, but

[27] Dorothy Norman, ed., "From the Writings and Conversations of Alfred Stieglitz," *Twice a Year*, 1 (Fall-Winter 1938), 77-110.

[28] *Ibid.*, 110.

[29] Quoted in Norman, *Stieglitz*, 27.

[30] *Ibid.*, 28.

simply *am*, then I may be said to be truly affirming life. Not to *know*, but to let exist what is, that alone, perhaps, is truly to know,"[31] because "the subconscious pushing through the conscious, driven by an urge coming from beyond its own knowing, its own control; trying to live in the light, like the seed pushing up through the earth —will alone have roots, can alone be fertile."[32] "When I photograph I make love," Stieglitz used to say.

It is of course obvious that several of the seeds of Stieglitz's thought lie in the ideas of the Transcendentalists. It is significant that Stieglitz and his entourage chose to inherit some of the fundamental concepts of the first indigenous American intellectual movement; although Stieglitz's affinity was closer to Whitman than to the Transcendentalists proper.[33] Stieglitz, however, was instrumental in defining, through his photographs, a practical means by which the American artist could move himself into his native surroundings and express himself in terms of his own local experience. In 1915 de Zayas could still say: "American artists have always had before them an inner censorship formed by an exotic education. They do not see their surroundings at first hand. They do not understand their milieu." And, he therefore argued, "the real American life is still unexpressed. America remains to be discovered." De Zayas thought at the time that although "Stieglitz wanted to

---

[31] *Ibid.*, 54.

[32] "From the Writings and Conversations of Alfred Stieglitz," 77.

[33] Whitman had said: "I will make the poems of materials, for I think they are to be the most spiritual poems." In quoting this line, Waldo Frank, in *Our America* (New York 1919), remarked that it showed the difference between Whitman and Emerson: "The difference between strength and weakness: between the mystic whose Mystery is the consciousness of All, and the mystic whose Mystery is escape" (p. 71).

103

work this miracle," he had failed.[34] But de Zayas was an outsider himself, one of the "foreign influences." While respecting and admiring the achievements of European art deeply, Stieglitz primarily used those foreign influences, in de Zayas' own words, "as supports for finding an expression of the conception of American life," which could then be used to develop a truly American art. That is why, just when de Zayas felt Stieglitz had failed, Stieglitz, in fact, had succeeded in creating the remarkable nucleus of artists and writers who under his aegis, and guided at least partly by his beliefs, set out to create the first unified and truly successful, consciously American art movement.

Williams was one of those who eagerly listened to Stieglitz through the years, as he explained his ideas about the nature and purpose of artistic expression and pointed to the need for an indigenous American art. Even when the poet came to write his negative memorial to Stieglitz, he had to admit that he had admired the photographer deeply "as an intelligence, as a profound prophet of real values as opposed to the murderous falsity of cash over everything else, as a pioneer photographer, as a friend, as a lover of peace and as a fighter."[35] And in the preface to his *Autobiography* he felt sufficiently contrite about his summary treatment of his relationship with Stieglitz to reaffirm his debt to the man. "For instance," Williams points out in that preface, "I'd go to see Alfred Stieglitz. I did this fairly regularly at one time. There'd be no one at all in the gallery. He'd recognize me, and after I had had a chance to look around he'd come out from behind his partition and

[34] Marius de Zayas in 291, 5-6 (July-August 1915).
[35] William Carlos Williams, "What of Alfred Stieglitz?" unpublished ms., Yale University Library, Collection of American Literature.

we'd begin to talk. We'd talk about the pictures, about John Marin and what he was doing then. Or another day it would be a Hartley show or a visit to the Portinari show at the Modern Museum. Or we'd have been to hear Pablo Casals. Or we'd visit the tapestries at the Cloisters. After that I'd come home and think—that is to say, to scribble. I'd scribble for days, sometimes, after such a visit, or even years, it might be, trying to discover how my mind had readjusted itself to its contacts."[36]

After such meetings with Stieglitz, or others: "Time meant nothing to me. I might be in the middle of some flu epidemic, the phone ringing day and night, madly, not a moment free. That made no difference. If the fit was on me—if something Stieglitz or Kenneth [Burke] had said was burning inside me, having bred there overnight demanding outlet—I would be like a woman at term; no matter what else was up, that demand had to be met."[37]

It was Stieglitz who, for Williams as well as for the painters, provided the essential example of the means by which the artist could reach out to a new, more accurate mode of representing the world of experience. If Stieglitz was a pioneer in American art, it was primarily because he established the basis for a non-metaphoric art in America. Until Stieglitz began to emphasize the object in his photographs, the artists in this country had been overwhelmingly concerned only with those qualities in reality which were representative of indirect experience. In the wake of the settlers and immigrants, the American artist in the nineteenth century had spent all his efforts in turning the native reality into a shadow of experience informed by the European object. His American landscapes were landscapes distorted by the vision

[36] *Autobiography*, xii-xiii.
[37] *Ibid.*, xiii.

of Claude Lorrain, his poems were about Indian burying grounds, not as they really were, but as they might have been if placed on an English heath, amid the castles of the gothic imagination. For Stieglitz and his followers the immediate task was to restore the integrity of the American object, to perceive it free from metaphor, to see it as it actually existed, within its own experimental framework. They struggled to free the American object from the impositions of alien consciousness, from the metaphoric vision which forces the object to become other than itself, and hence be continually misapprehended. There can be no doubt that Williams was profoundly influenced by what Stieglitz and the painters set out to do. What is even Williams' extensive campaign in favor of the word as a "thing itself" if not an extension of these concepts? For Stieglitz, as well as for Williams, the breakthrough of the European painters had been a profound initial catalyst. But Stieglitz, from the very beginning, had a fundamental understanding of, an intellectual affinity to, the attitudes which these painters had developed, an understanding and affinity which Williams and most other Americans lacked. He saw, moreover, how the concepts of the European artists would have to be modified in order to become useful in the United States. He chose and molded his associates accordingly. He was primarily an intuitive artist and was by no means willing to spend much time in writing down his ideas. He expressed himself largely in long discussions with his friends. Carl Zigrosser once remarked, "most often he [wrote] his scripture not on paper, but on the minds and feelings of men and women." It remained therefore to his literary disciples to mold his ideas into theoretical disquisitions, just as the painters were interpreting his concepts along their own lines, on canvas. The writers who did so most effectively were

Waldo Frank, Marsden Hartley (in his guise of *littérateur*), and especially Paul Rosenfeld. Their critical writings best define the "American" qualities which unify the otherwise quite individual and disparate artistic achievements of the artists of the Stieglitz group. Williams read their essays avidly, and echoed them closely when he came to write his own book about the American experience, *In the American Grain.*

IV. THE EVANGELISTS OF THE AMERICAN MOMENT

*t*HROUGHOUT the Twenties it was common in literary circles to associate Williams with the Stieglitz group. Gorham Munson, in *Destinations* (1928), pointed to the poet's close association with the photographer and with the writers of *The Seven Arts*; in 1929, in *The Rediscovery of America*, Waldo Frank mentioned him as one of the "apocalyptic artists" around Stieglitz. Stieglitz, Frank felt, was "perhaps the most American of all, since the substance of man's apocalyptic vision is *recorded nature* and since his tool is a machine."[1]

It was probably during the days of *The Seven Arts* that Williams first became acquainted with Paul Rosenfeld, perhaps at 291. Rosenfeld, by that time, had already become the official theoretician of 291, as he was to be of its subsequent incarnations. Williams, even in the unlikely event that he never did visit the gallery, could not have avoided exposure to the essentials of Stieglitz's philosophy, through *Camera Work*, through Rosenfeld, and through his friendship with Demuth, Hartley, and Kreymborg. The special features of the photographer's ideas about art—the fact that at 291 and in *Camera Work* America had for the first time "really been re-expressed in terms of America without the outside influence of Paris art-schools or their dilute offspring"[2]— may not have struck Williams as of primary importance during the years of his first excitement over Cubism and the other new European art movements. There can be

[1] Waldo Frank, *The Rediscovery of America* (New York 1929), 140.

[2] Paul Strand, "Photography," *The Seven Arts* (August 1917), 524-26.

no doubt, however, that toward 1917, at a time when he felt that the "reawakening of letters" which had been taking place from 1913 on, "was being blotted out by the war,"[3] Rosenfeld's resolute espousal of the need for American values in art must have had a strong appeal to him.

Another admirer of Stieglitz whom Williams met around this time was Charles Sheeler, who, like Rosenfeld, was to become a lifelong friend of the poet. He often went to see Hartley in his studio, and one night, at Lola Ridge's, Williams recalls, "Hartley, whose pictures, along with those of Demuth and Sheeler, I always went to see, brought a young man with him named Robert McAlmon."[4] With McAlmon he started his magazine *Contact* in December 1920, publishing in the second issue a prose sketch of Matisse's painting "The Blue Nude," which would seem to contain a reference to 291: "On the French grass, in that room on Fifth ave., lay that woman who had never seen my poor land."[5] As a reader of, and contributor to, *The Dial*, Williams studied Rosenfeld's important essays on Stieglitz and American painting, and he probably visited the photographer himself quite regularly at his rooms, discussing with him such matters as Hartley's book, *Adventures in the Arts*, of which, as we have seen, Stieglitz had per-

[3] *Autobiography*, 158.
[4] *Ibid.*, 171.
[5] Reprinted in *Selected Essays*, 30-31. If Williams did refer to 291 here, as seems likely, his memory even at this time may not have been serving him well. The "Blue Nude" was shown at the Armory Show, but there is no indication that it was ever shown at 291 or anywhere else in New York during the 1910's. What may have confused Williams is that a reproduction of the painting in question was published in *Camera Work*, in the special issue of 1912 which contained Gertrude Stein's articles on Matisse and Picasso. Williams almost certainly saw this issue and probably even owned a copy.

sonally sent him a copy. When Rosenfeld took on the editorship of *Manuscripts* he included two poems by Williams in the first issue. *Manuscripts* was very much an underground publication, much like Williams' own *Contact*, and was distinctly a "house organ" of the Stieglitz group, financed by its contributors. Rosenfeld at the same time published articles on Hartley, Dove, and O'Keeffe in *Vanity Fair*, and began to write the rest of the material which would ultimately be collected in his *Port of New York* (1924). This volume of essays was almost entirely devoted to the members of the Stieglitz group. Carl Sandburg, also at this time associated with the photographer, and Williams were the only poets whose work Rosenfeld deemed sufficiently representative of the values he was looking for to find a place in the book. When, in 1923, McAlmon's Contact Editions published a volume of Hartley's poetry, at about the same time it brought out Williams' *Spring and All*, Hartley wrote to Stieglitz from Berlin, praising Williams and observing that he had certainly made "a splendid struggle to plasticize all his various selves."[6] If Williams was successful in that struggle, then certainly his success was in large measure due to his careful study of the writings of the Stieglitz group.

The ideas presented in these writings are clear-cut, but they are scattered among numerous short essays, and often it is fruitful to combine the comments of several authors, to establish the common core of attitudes which linked them with Stieglitz. Paul Strand, for instance, a photographer himself, and for many years one of Stieglitz's most devoted followers, in an article about his mentor in *Broom*, outlined the origin of what was perhaps the most central value for all these men: the moment of

[6] Unpublished letter to Stieglitz, October 9, 1923, Stieglitz Archive, Yale.

experience, caught and recorded, to become, through the objective delineation of organic forms, an equivalence, not just a record, of that experience. "The camera," Strand says, echoing Stieglitz:

". . . can hold in a unique way, a moment. If the moment be a living one for the photographer, that is, if it be significantly related to other moments in his experience, and he knows how to put that relativety into form, he may do with a machine what the human brain and hand, through the act of memory cannot do. So perceived the whole concept of a portrait takes on a new meaning, that of a record of innumerable elusive and constantly changing states of being, manifested physically. This is as true of all objects as of the human object. With the eye of the machine, Stieglitz has recorded just that, has shown that the portrait of an individual is really the sum of a hundred or more photographs. He has looked with three eyes and has been able to hold, by purely photographic means, space filling, tonality and tactility, line and form, that moment when the forces at work in a human being become most intensely physical and objective. In thus revealing the spirit of the individual he has documented the world of that individual, which is today."[7]

Thus, in following Stieglitz the artist could establish a sense of meaningful relationship between person and object which did not make the object subservient to the emotions it was to express, but equivalent: "In the abstract relations of these shapes, tones and lines, caught in a particular moment and held, [Stieglitz] was expressing equivalents of human relationship and feeling."[8]

[7] Paul Strand, "Photography and the New God," *Broom*, III, 4 (November 1922), 252-8.

[8] Paul Strand, "Stieglitz, An Appraisal," *Popular Photography*, XXI, 1 (July 1947), 62, 88-98.

Waldo Frank's *Our America* (1919) also bears the Stieglitz stamp. To Frank, 291 was "a religious fact," a "miracle." It was "an altar where talk was often loud, heads never bared, but where no lie and no compromise could live. A little altar at which life was worshipped above the noise of a dead city."[9] Stieglitz, he felt, had "mastered the dominant details of industrial life," and had made them "serve the unifying vision of human spirit. At a time when Europe was still groping toward it [he] had found the true *abstract* of art:—not in the avoidance of representation nor in the ignoring of detail, but in their mastery and fusion to an essential vision." He had "mastered a deep reality and lifted it up to his own terms" (181). Frank's language has the peculiar mystic-idealistic tone of the prose of many in the 291 group, including Stieglitz himself. It is a language which is itself strikingly American in its rambling, enthusiastic stridency. Words such as vision, spirit, the "sanctity of art" tend to obscure to present-day readers the fact that the idealism of these men was grounded solidly in objective reality, and consisted mainly of a positive belief in the potential beauty of life and mankind, as well as in the communicative, educational power of art. An idealism which sought its sources beyond life was anathema to them: "We believe we are the true realists," Frank said, "we who insist that in the essence of all reality lies the ideal. America is for us indeed a promise and a dream. But only because we are sure that in discovering and controlling the complex conditions of our land, we shall find inviolate within them the promise and dream whereof I speak" (9).

If the promise of America were to be made real, America would have to be discovered in terms of itself. "The

[9] *Our America* (New York 1919), 184. Page numbers in the text refer to this edition.

112

problem is . . . to lift America into self-knowledge that shall be luminous so that she may shine, vibrant so that she may be articulate" (5). To make America know itself was not to follow the transcendental escape, "but to go to the basic materials of life, not to conceive over-whelming panoramas of power and industry encompass-ing the entire country, but to identify with one's native ground, to try to attune oneself to a place rather than to the expanse of a nation: The lowly Mexican is articu-late, the lordly American is not. For the Mexican has really dwelt with his soil, cultivated his spirit in it, not alone his maize. He has stooped to conquer" (96). The Indian, "whether he dwelt in populous cities or in *tepees* . . . , lived in a spiritual world so true and so profound, that the heel of the pioneer has even now not wholly stamped it out" (109). The one painter who, in the past, had been able to capture something of the inner correspondence between his spirit and his native ground had been Albert P. Ryder, although even Ryder had been "too near the transcendentalists in intellectual interest. A part of him had a way of flying off from an opaque world into translucent aether" (156). Yet, because "another part of him—his eyes—was enamored of the sea, studied the matter of the clouds, grasped the secret of New England landscapes," he became the great American painter. "The world to him was massive, dense and real. . . . His will was to recapture the reality of life" (157).

Sense of place therefore was a prerequisite to the development of any coherent sense of America as a whole. Marsden Hartley, in his *Adventures in the Arts*, a volume of essays published in 1921, but consisting largely of pieces written and published in the 1910's, insisted that an artist could not hope to be effective unless he had established an elemental relationship

113

between himself and his native soil. For him too, Stieglitz had been a major catalyst: "Here was one man who believed in another man over a space of more than twenty years," he said in 1934. "The thing that happened [at 291] was found to be a high and strictly pure American value, and an American contribution to American cultivation. The purpose of Alfred Stieglitz and the famous little room 291 through which I was permitted to enter and pass onward to a given realization which I am still engaged in completing, is as genuine today as it was twenty-five years ago, when we all entered into its trust and were given credence." In those early years, Hartley said, "I only knew I had had some kind of definite experience with nature, the nature of my own native land. I could only tell at what I had been looking and from whom my release had come. Steichen's remark to Stieglitz then was, I don't see, Stieglitz, what you see in those pictures, why you bothered about them, or him, there is nothing there."[10]

Spurred on by Stieglitz's approval and support as well as his example, Hartley, in *Adventures in the Arts*, emphasized first of all that the artist, in order to establish his relationship with his surroundings, must devote himself intensely and continuously to a study of contemporary things: "I am related to the world by the way I feel attached to the life of it as exemplified in the vividness of the moment."[11] Once this relationship has been established the artist can begin to acquire, like the "Red Man," "the calm of all our native earth," for "it is from the earth all things arise" (27). Like Frank, Hartley

[10] Marsden Hartley, "291-And the Brass Bowl," in *America and Alfred Stieglitz*, edited by Waldo Frank, Dorothy Norman et al. (New York 1934), 240-41.

[11] Marsden Hartley, *Adventures in the Arts* (New York 1921), 8. Subsequent page numbers refer to this edition.

took the Indian as exemplary of the truly native artist: "It is nature that gives him the sign and symbol for the expression of life as a synthesis" (18). As a result "he is the living embodiment in color of various tonal characteristics of the landscape around him. He knows the harmonic value of a bark or a hide, or a bit of broken earth, and of the natural unpolluted coloring to be drawn out of various types of vegetable matter at his disposal" (20). Man's spiritual origins as well as his tools for expression lie in the earth on which he lives. Therefore the American artist, if he is to express life, must, as Cézanne did, strive "toward actualities, toward the realization of beauty as it is seen to exist in the real, in the object itself, whether it be mountain or apple or human, the entire series of living things in relation to one another" (30). Cézanne painted "not cold studies of inanimate things," but "pulsing realizations of living substances striving toward each other, lending each other their individual activities" (33). But in order to establish the objective relationships between things, the artist must not attempt, as Walt Whitman did, "to catalogue in detail the entire obvious universe." He should rather be "engrossed with the idea of simplification, directness and an easy relationship of the elements selected for presentation to each other" (34). The first requisite toward this necessary process of simplification is that the artist identify with a specific place, preferably the region in which he was born. Hartley, like Frank, believed that in this sense Ryder was as yet "our finest genius, the most creative, the most racial," for his was "a personality unrelated to anything other than itself, an imagination belonging strictly to our soil and specifically to our Eastern geography" (40). Ryder was "conscious of nothing really outside of native associations and native deductions." Although it may come as a surprise to many people, Hartley said, "art in general

115

is more national or local now than it has ever been" (57), and he pointed out that Maurice de Vlaminck's claim that "art is local," is "just as true of America as any other country," and that there is an art, largely undiscovered as yet, "which is peculiar to our specific temper and localized sensibility" (60). To return to a sense of place in art, however, is by no means to discard one's awareness of international artistic movements. The better an artist's comprehension of the universal implications of his art, "the more local it becomes," and "the truer it will be to the place in which it is produced" (62). In fact, if one loses sight of the larger realities inherent in one's observation of place, if place does not come to represent the universal qualities in man, if, in other words, we fail to express the universal through the local, the artist fails and becomes a mere regionalist, a "local colorist." That is what happened to Winslow Homer: "His mind was too local. There is nothing of universal appeal in him" (47). Among the artists who at the close of the 1910's best represented the concept of "localized expression" according to Hartley, were all the painters of the Stieglitz group, as well as certain others, such as Stanton Macdonald Wright, Man Ray, and Stuart Davis, all of whom had some connection with 291. Moreover, Hartley emphasized, "the three modern photographers Alfred Stieglitz, Charles Sheeler and Paul Strand must be included."

The First World War showed, Hartley believed, that the painter could not, needed not, look to Paris any more for inspiration: "It is having its pronounced effect upon the creative powers of the individual in all countries, almost obliging him to create his own impulse upon his own soil" (241). But until he finally settled down, Hartley was in many ways too much the restless traveler, too much without a native soil, to be considered by the other members of the 291 group as fully representative of the localized art he advocated. He was indeed the only one of Stieglitz's protégés toward whose work Paul Rosenfeld always retained a certain reservation, and that may very well have meant that these reservations were Stieglitz's as well, for, as Edmund Wilson has remarked about his friend, Rosenfeld "stood in something like a filial relation" to the photographer, and the 291 group "became for him both family and church." And, Wilson continued, somewhat jealously, it would seem: "his range as a writer on the plastic arts was limited by the exclusiveness of his interest in the work of the Stieglitz group. It was difficult, if not impossible, to persuade him to pay attention to any contemporary American painter who was not a protégé of Stieglitz's, and if Stieglitz had excommunicated a refractory or competitive disciple, Paul, following the official directive, would condemn him not merely as an artist, but as a reprobate who had somehow commited an unpardonable moral treason."[12]

In 1921 and 1922, Rosenfeld published a series of articles in *The Dial* and *Vanity Fair* on American painting, on some of the painters in the 291 group and on Stieglitz. These essays formed the core for his book *Port of New York*, published in 1924, and together they constitute the most completely developed theoretical discussion of the practices and aims of the artists in the Stieglitz group. *Port of New York* remains an important and central statement about the American artist's need for identity and his progress towards its acquisition, but the earlier essays are more spontaneous,[13] and often more assertive.

[12] Edmund Wilson, "Paul Rosenfeld: Three Phases," in *Paul Rosenfeld: Voyager in the Arts*, edited by Jerome Mellquist and Lucie Wiese (New York 1948), 7.

[13] For instance, the "dirt" in the 1921 essay on Stieglitz turns into "soilure" in *Port of New York*.

Like the others, Rosenfeld believed that with Ryder "for the first time, paintings speak to the American of what lies between him and his native soil," but he also felt that, although Ryder had "succeeded in digging down through sand to the sea" there is an essential flaw in his work which is indeed representative of a flaw in the consciousness of nearly all Americans, namely, the refusal to regard life in terms of its locality and the significance of the present. "We of the new world," Rosenfeld asked, "do we not all of us strain away into some dim land?" The American, and especially the American artist, believes he can find inspiration and significant form in exotic worlds, fairy lands, and impossible adventure; he does not dare, or does not care to face, "the world of humdrum familiar things." All the American admires is "the otherwhere, the far unseen." The sun, which lights up the objects of the natural world in real and accurate sharpness of line, volume, and meaning, "annihilates us quite." Only in the dim illumination of moonlight can the American see beauty in buildings, stones and grit. He needs to dilute reality with fancy to accept it. Ryder had to cast moonlight over the soil and sky he had just discovered. Even the work of artists such as Hartley "still reflects the American incompleteness." Hartley, although he searches to express himself in terms of the objects in reality, withdraws, like others, such as Max Weber and Stanton Macdonald Wright, into intellectualism. None of these artists can "breast the moment quite nakedly."[14] Hartley manages, in fact, often to catch some of the essence of things, but his success is incomplete because he "has not immersed himself sufficiently

[14] Paul Rosenfeld, "American Painting," *The Dial*, LXXI, 6 (December 1921), 649-70.

deeply in his material. He has not been able to lose himself in his 'object.' "[15]

To capture reality, to understand the meaning of his spiritual constitution, the artist must feel deeply and see clearly and without prejudice, until the object opens itself to him in its full visual and tactile purity, revealing in its constitution the objective equivalence of the emotion which moves the artist. The artist then becomes the recording agent. His subjective response is made universal when it becomes absorbed by the object whose texture, line, color, and volume represent the elements which evoked the artist's original emotion. The artist must now arrange his canvas in terms of those qualities of texture, line, and color, objectively seen. Thus we witness in the artist's work "the circling of interest between his own breast and the thing before him, with the result that the thing before him begets for him an importance quite as great as his own person, and is perceived, a life with rights identical to his own; the circling that continues uninterruptedly round and round till the man almost becomes a transparency through which the light of life streams, till the man almost becomes the thing before him and the thing the man." But a painter like Marsden Hartley insists too much on intellectual analysis, and this removes him from the object he is studying, rather than making that object "visible to him as being an integral portion of the chain of which he is himself a link, and like him a material in which the informing spirit of the universe stirs."[16]

Ultimately, because his emotional constitution is determined by the forms and conditions of the material world into which he was born, the artist must return

[15] Paul Rosenfeld, "The Paintings of Marsden Hartley," *Vanity Fair*, xviii (August 1922), 47, 84, 94, 96.
[16] *Ibid.*, 84.

to this material world to express his emotions. If he has learned how to see clearly, unencumbered by intellectual fantasies, he will recognize the elements which are the source of his feelings, in the objects of that world. By selecting and juxtaposing appropriate objects or by abstracting their salient forms, lines, and volumes, the artist can transmit his emotions by means of the universal "spiritual" qualities inherent in the objects. But he must take special care that the objects he records retain their autonomy as things. They should never come to stand for something else; if they take on a metaphorical quality the artist has lost sight of their objective meaning as real things in a real world—as metaphor they become part of the constructs of the intellect and cannot be regarded as things in themselves, for themselves.

Yet in Hartley's work this is exactly what too often still happens, the object too often still remains a tool: It has "in some fashion remained always subordinate to the worker." This, Rosenfeld argues, is indeed the central element which keeps artists in America from creating an indigenous art. The American tries to escape the moment and is not content to "sit and watch three trees growing in the yard before his house," but rather hunts for "the past, the future, Europe and Asia, the Wild West and the opium-tainted East."[17] His great sin is his refusal to take account of the earth on which he lives. Hartley, like such artists as Kenneth Hayes Miller and Arthur B. Davies, suffers from "the fault of the society in which he grew." Moreover, like these men, he still "had the transcendental strain in his blood, always felt the distance more beautiful than the near." He, like most

[17] "American Painting," 654.

other Americans, had a "yearning tendency left in him by puritan and pioneer forebears."[18] For Hartley,

"The relation he bears his object is one that is very typical of the American in his general contacts, resulting, it would seem, from the attitude taken by the whole of society to the soil which nourishes it. The men who have really loved the earth they have worked in America have been rare. The feeling for the earth which is character- istic of the peasantry of the older countries, the sense that it is an organism like themselves, which has to be nourished and developed and enriched and cared for so that it will increase, the whole desire that makes 'grow' the soil, that, has been felt in this land until recent times only by the poor Indian. His dances and rituals were motivated very much by the knowledge that if he put himself in harmony with nature, nature would put her- self in harmony with him. But the Yankee, it is a com- mon fact, has always ravished the earth. He has always approached it with the wish to get from it with little effort what he could, and not to give as much as he got. There has been no love in his intercourse with it. He has wanted to get away from it, to rise 'above' it. And that attitude has repeated itself throughout his civiliza- tion as a figure in a rug. He is not the husbandman of machinery any more than he is the husbandman of the earth. And in his art, he withholds himself no otherwise."[19]

The American, then, refuses to see the natural world in its own terms. He does not realize that to grow spirit- ually he must partake of the organic structure of his native soil; only then will he be able to understand and express his own most profound emotions. Hartley knows

[18] *Ibid.*, 655.
[19] "The Paintings of Marsden Hartley," 84.

this and has been searching for his proper contact with the moment; in his paintings, indeed, there is "a voluptuous life of the touch." But if he is ever to achieve his purest expression, there is only one thing for him to do: "Some day, perhaps some day not so far distant, Hartley will have to go back to Maine. For it seems that flight from Maine is in part flight from his deep feelings." He must return there, for there only, among the trees and mountain walls, can he get truly "the sense of his own existence."[20]

Hartley, of course, continued to wander for a number of years after Rosenfeld had written these remarks, but finally he did go back to Maine, the intuitive artist winning out over the intellectual in him. Meanwhile, in discussing Hartley and other "faulted" artists such as Albert Pinkham Ryder and Max Weber, Rosenfeld set down very clearly the concepts which guided the Stieglitz group in their search for an art expressive of their "moment," of their own time and place: if the artist in America were only able to establish a close relationship between himself and the immediate objective world around him, if he were only truly locally oriented in his vision of the materials of life, he would automatically become an American artist. For the soil, the trees, the ugliness and beauty of industry and machinery, all the elements which would of needs constitute a truly American existence, would then speak through his work, and create for him the identity which most of his fellow citizens seemed intent upon eradicating. But in order to succeed in establishing that identity, the artist must take the utmost care to speak through the objects themselves, to let them keep their autonomy, their non-metaphoric, real, organic solidity, their absolute, self-contained meaning as objects. Otherwise he would fall into the amorphous mass of

[20] *Ibid.*, 96.

callous opportunists which constituted the soulless, rootless American populace. These people had no eyes for the land they lived on, or even for the houses and skyscrapers they lived in. They would destroy without qualm a primeval forest because the wood might make them rich. They were so blind to the land through which they traveled that they needed flashing electric lights to see the harsh diner jutting incongruously out of a desert landscape. They were blind also to the devastating ugliness of trash-piled empty city lots and the chaotic rambling slums around them; they hardly noticed that the building put up just recently was already cracking. America had always meant to them the place to make a fortune, not the place on which they stood. America, the land of immigrants, was not the land of birth, of origin. And as the undiscovered ranges of the continent opened up to the children of the immigrants, they too did not bother to establish a contact with the soil. Thus where in most other countries art and literature were automatically an expression of the earth and of the materials which formed the artist's contact with the objects of his local environment, the American artist had always felt compelled to work with second-hand materials, because to reject contact with his native soil was the only "tradition" his experience recognized. Instead of looking to his own environment for inspiration he tried to use the soil, nature, history, and attitudes of other cultures; as a result his art remained still-born, his work a miserable imitation of art.

The members of the Stieglitz group argued that because the intuitive contact between humanity and his native soil had been rooted out of the American consciousness, the artist who wished to be truly American would have to make a conscious effort to reestablish that contact. This could be done only by going back to the

123

very basis of nature, the object. All concrete forms, natural as well as man-made, should be seen in terms of their relationship to the artist, and the artist should establish from the things about him the meaning of his own existence. By transmitting what he saw as accurately as possible in terms of his individual vision, he would then be able to inculcate an awareness of the universal emotions underlying the materials of his environment to his fellow Americans, while yet reflecting the specific elements of his local consciousness.

The Stieglitz group was quite insistent that in advocating this return to a direct attention for the position of the object as such within nature it reestablished a concept of objective realism which had nothing to do with the familiar romantic concept of a return to nature. Rather, they felt, they were advocating an attitude which, it is true, had been lost through the development of industrialism, but which had none of the vague generalized sentimentality which guided the response of a city-bred person taking a trip out into the country and heaving sighs over the exquisite beauty of it all. Indeed, what they were advocating was the obverse of escapism, an attention only to *things as they are.* The city-bred artist should explore the objects of the city, as they are, and attend to the materials of "wild" nature only when he found himself living in "wild" nature. For those artists whose consciousness had not been disassociated from the reality amidst which they lived—the Hebrew poets, the medieval painters, Homer and most Oriental artists— the objects of nature meant more than romanticized panoramas of nature ever could. They did not care for pastoral scenes as such but for the grit of the soil. For them seeing the rain soak into newly plowed soil was equivalent to all of life; they found an objective equivalent to the emotion of love in the texture of wet black earth. "The Chinese," said Rosenfeld, "knew themselves intergrown with all creation, knew no thing not intergrown with them, and their wisdom symbolized itself in the completeness . . . of their expressions."[21] Consciousness of the matter of existence was self-consciousness, and that, as Rosenfeld had remarked already in *The Seven Arts* in 1916, was exactly what Stieglitz wanted to give America.

To Rosenfeld, indeed, Stieglitz was the purest example of an artist in tune with his time and his country. In him the local was truly expressed in universal terms. "Save for Whitman there has been among us no native-born artist equal to this photographer," he said in 1921. The machine succeeded during the nineteenth century in reducing most of humanity to spiritual inertia and caused man to "seek to regard objects only with the eyes of commerce and industry, and not with those of the earth-loving, nature-loving, green-and-growth loving spirit," but Stieglitz reversed that process and made the machine once more serve the human spirit. One "of the great affirmers of life," he showed with his camera that "there seems to be scarcely anything, any object, in all the world without high import, scarcely anything that is not in some way related to himself. The humblest objects appear to be, for him, instinct with marvellous life." For him "the dirt of an unwashed window pane, a brick wall, a piece of tattered matting" was as important as a sunset. "He has found universal, found forming a related design, the wheelrims and the sides of carts, sign-painted walls, the stormlight of a feverish afternoon in New York," and he has shown us how in human beings "the life of the pores, of the hairs along the shin-bone, of the veining of the pulse and the liquid moisture on the upper lip" represent more profoundly than a pano-

[21] *Ibid.*, 84.

ramic view ever could "the very natural forces which have created man, and which he, in turn, is striving fitfully to make part of his body." By registering "what [lay] between himself and the object" he affirmed life, because each of his photographs proclaimed "the majesty of the moment, the augustness of the here, the now." With his camera he met his environment "on its terms, and at the same time, on his own"; through his pictures "we see—not Stieglitz, but America, New York, ourselves."[22]

[22] Paul Rosenfeld, "Alfred Stieglitz," *The Dial,* LXX (April 1921), 397-409.

V. DOCTOR WILLIAMS AND
  THE NEW WORLD

*t*HE WRITINGS of Rosenfeld, Hartley, and Frank develop the basic implications of Stieglitz's main ideas, and as such they form a very useful extension of the photographer's personal influence over the artists who wanted to develop a truly American form of expression. Among these, Williams, who read, looked, and listened very carefully, was certainly one of the most prominent.

Williams had early felt the urge to express himself in terms of his American background. When he saw Isadora Duncan in 1908 he was tremendously impressed by her performance, the more because she was "one of our own people." The performance made him feel, he wrote his brother, "doubly strengthened in my desire and my determination to accomplish my part in our wonderful future."[1] But Williams was also "very late, very slow, to find out about the world,"[2] and in his earliest writings he gave very little indication that he had found a way in which to approach that world. In the meantime he discovered the significance of European painting and began to apply its implications to his work. Yet while he was still struggling with abstraction, he began to realize that the intellect was of doubtful use to him as a poet, because as his work grew more abstract, more disjointed, it began to lose its link with the real world, the world of sense impressions. Thus even while he learned about the elements of the real world in his examination of European painting, he began to discover, with the painters of

[1] Unpublished letter to Edgar Williams, October 21, 1908, Lockwood Memorial Library, State University of New York at Buffalo.
[2] I Wanted To Write a Poem, 33.

127

the Stieglitz group, that abstraction would lead him away from a truly American statement of the world. In a short essay, "America, Whitman and the Art of Poetry," published in 1917, he discussed Whitman in terms of the paintings of J.M.W. Turner and pointed out that "the splendor of [Whitman's] pigment blends his work into some semblance of unity." But he also stressed that verse must have an organizing principle: "without comprehension there will be little unfolding."[3] It is significant that he credited Charles Demuth with having originated this observation. It was by now obvious to Williams, as to Demuth, that the objective world should supply the pigment, the organizing principle, for any viable form of indigenous American expression. The elements of the new verse form, Williams began to argue, should not court complete abstraction, they "must be perfectly concrete or they will escape through the fingers."[4] With the artists of the Stieglitz group he decided, as he stated in the introduction to *Kora in Hell*, that "the true value is that peculiarity which gives an object a character by itself. The associational or sentimental value is false." Therefore metaphor should not be part of the artist's tools. "Much more keen is that power which discovers in things those inimitable particles of dissimilarity to all other things which are the peculiar perfections of the thing in question." The thing itself should be the basis for all scrutiny. That very fact makes it clear that the artist should take account of the world directly around him. For "those who permit their senses to be despoiled of things under their noses by stories of all manner of things removed and unattainable are of frail imagination."

Thus toward the closing years of the 1910's many ideas

[3] In *Poetry Journal*, VIII, 1 (November 1917), 27-36.
[4] *Ibid.*, 30.

associated with the Stieglitz group were beginning to blend with influences from the European painters in Williams' writings. As he moved closer to the central concerns of 291, he began to link his notions about "the thing itself" with the implications of Stieglitz's concept of place. In *The Little Review* he criticized the "war poems" of Richard Aldington and D. H. Lawrence as "empty nonsense having no relation to the place or time they were written in. They have no existence."[5] In *Poetry* he defined facts as "the fundamental emotional basis of all knowledge."[6] At the time of the publication of the first issue of *Contact* in December 1920, Williams was talking very much in the terminology of the artists around Stieglitz: "He who does not know his own world, in whatever confused form it may be, must either stupidly fail to learn from foreign work or stupidly swallow it without knowing how to judge of its essential value." Therefore the artist must pay "attention to the immediacy of [his] own contact," and "become awake to his own locality."[7]

It is perhaps useful to emphasize at this point that Williams during this time, as throughout his career as a poet, was influenced by numerous sources in both literature and art. Like most other "avant garde" writers, he had been profoundly impressed by the installments of Joyce's *Ulysses* in *The Little Review*. European movements in literature and art, such as Dadaism and later Surrealism, fascinated him and influenced the structure of his verse. As his work developed, however, such influences tended to take the form of superficial, even modish,

---

[5] William Carlos Williams, "Four Foreigners," *The Little Review*, VI, 5 (September 1919), 36-39.

[6] William Carlos Williams, "Notes From a Talk on Poetry," *Poetry*, XIV (July 1919), 211-16.

[7] *Selected Essays*, 28.

adaptations of his manner of presentation to styles currently *en vogue*. They usually failed to provoke significant changes in the focus underlying his work. Williams, after all, was committed to "making it new." It would be misleading, however, to overemphasize these secondary elements. They were of relatively minor importance, in the development of Williams' poetics, in comparison with his initial fascination with Cubism, and his subsequent central preoccupation with the close observation of the objects and materials of the real world—the development, in other words, of his concept of objectivism. The structure of Williams' *Spring and All* (1923), for instance, its pattern of alternating sections of prose and poetry, shows the continuing influence of the European painters, further modified by the example of Joyce and others. In both the prose and the poetry the fragmentation Williams learned from the Cubists, and was to continue to use throughout his life, plays a very important role. But at the same time the poet's basic concern as an artist has clearly shifted toward the careful delineation and presentation of objects. Especially in the substance of Williams' remarks in the important prose sections of *Spring and All* the influence of Rosenfeld's articles on Stieglitz and American painting and Hartley's *Adventures in the Arts* becomes strikingly evident. Williams drew liberally on their work in his attempts to define an American poetry whose function would be analogous to the American painting that was being developed by the Stieglitz group.

Williams, in fact, specifically refers to *Adventures in the Arts* several times in *Spring and All*. Hartley had contributed to the first issue of *Contact*, and had undoubtedly taken an active part in the venture. He was clearly referring to *Contact* and the poets it published when he said in *Adventures in the Arts* that along with the "well defined grouping of younger painters working for a definitely localized idea of modernism," there was also "a grouping of poets in America who are adding new values to the English language, as well as assisting in the realization of a freshly evolved localized personality in modern poetics."[8]

Stieglitz and Hartley clearly inform the thought behind the opening sentences of *Spring and All*: "There is a constant barrier between the reader and his consciousness of immediate contact with the world." So does Rosenfeld: "If there is an ocean it is here. Or rather, the whole world is between: Yesterday, tomorrow, Europe, Asia, Africa—all things removed and impossible, the tower of the Church at Seville, the Parthenon."[9] These remarks directly recall Rosenfeld's "otherwheres." What the reader never seems to know, Williams continues, "and never dares to know is what he is at the exact moment that he is. And this moment is the only thing in which I am at all interested" (2). Stieglitz's belief in the moment and the now, so strongly emphasized by Hartley and Rosenfeld, here finds a place in Williams' poetic theory, side by side with the related concept of the supreme validity of the new which Williams had taken from Duchamp. Even Williams' language at this point takes on a quality very much like Stieglitz's: "Nearly all writing, up to the present, if not all art, has been especially designed to keep up the barrier between sense and the vaporous fringe which distracts the attention from its agonized approaches to the moment." Yet, "to refine, to clarify, to intensify that eternal moment in which we alone live," is exactly what we must do (3). This we can do only by going straight to the facts of

[8] *Adventures in the Arts*, 60.

[9] William Carlos Williams, *Spring and All* (Dijon, Contact Editions 1923), 1. Subsequent page references are to this edition.

reality. "Nothing," Williams emphasizes, "is put down in the present book—except through weakness of the imagination—which is not intended as of a piece with the 'nature' Shakespeare mentions and which Hartley speaks of so completely in his 'Adventures': it is the common thing which is anonymously about us" (21).

Again Williams emphasizes that to reach that "common thing," to make it meaningful, we must rid ourselves of the tendency to weigh it down with "crude symbolism," to turn it into metaphor. Williams felt that "every thing that I have done in the past—except those parts which may be called excellent—by chance, have that quality about them. It is typified by use of the word 'like' or that 'evocation' of the 'image' which served us for some time" (20). Instead, what the artist should do is "exactly what every eye must do with life, fix the particular with the universality of his own personality" (27). He must, in other words, find the universal in the object, or as Rosenfeld said in reference to Stieglitz, "fix the visual moments, register what lies between himself and the object before his lens at a given moment of time."[10]

To Williams this was clearly a function of the imagination, for by fixing the object and closely observing it in terms of its shapes and colors, the artist can "revaluate" it. Thus, by using "the forms common to experience," and moving them "from ordinary experience to the imagination," the artist can express himself in terms of real objects, "recognizable as the things touched by the hands during the day" (34), which when detached from their common environment become through their actual shapes representative of the universal qualities which the artist sees in them. The poet lets his imagination speak through his design, and this design can be effective only if it is based upon the materials of the real

[10] Rosenfeld, "Alfred Stieglitz," 400.

world. For, Williams stressed, as "Demuth and a few others do their best to point out . . . design is a function of the *imagination*, describing its movements, its colors," and does so in terms of the materials of the real world (16). That is why "the only realism in art is of the imagination. It is only thus that the work escapes plagiarism after nature and becomes a creation" (35). In this sense, a work of art, although it is formed out of the materials of the objective world, becomes a new, independent object, creating its own autonomous existence. The imagination, through design, can, if ideally operative, express all of experience in terms of a single visual object. That is why, as Williams remarked in *The Great American Novel*, published in the same year as *Spring and All*, there is "nothing more wonderful than to see the pears attached by their stems to the trees. Earth, trunk, branch, twig and the fruit: a circle soon to be completed when the pear falls."[11] It is of course exactly this sentiment which caused Stieglitz to take his photographs of apples on a bough. For "the only means" we have to give value to life, "is to recognize it with the imagination and name it" (41).

In the prose sections of *Spring and All* Williams tried to reach a synthesis between the intellectual values tending towards abstraction which he had taken from Europe, and his desire to discover the American object. Through American objects alone the American poet could express himself legitimately. Once Williams had reached that conclusion it was inevitable that he would consider his role as a poet analogous to that of the painters in the Stieglitz group, and the structure and content of his poetry began to show a clear dependence on their

[11] William Carlos Williams, *The Great American Novel* (1923), reprinted in *American Short Novels*, edited by R. P. Blackmur (New York 1960), 324.

definition of the visual reality of the American scene.

At the same time, as was only to be expected, Williams began to feel a need to "learn the essentials of the American situation,"[12] and to "find out for myself what the land of my more or less accidental birth might signify."[13] Williams locates the origin of this impulse towards the beginning of 1922, just after Rosenfeld's essays in *The Dial*, and concurrent with those on Hartley, Dove, and O'Keeffe in *Vanity Fair*. That these essays were a strong inspiration for what was to become *In the American Grain* is beyond doubt, because echoes of Rosenfeld's remarks about America and the American character can be found throughout the book. Sometimes, in fact, these echoes become so strong that they begin to take on the nature of quotations.

Agreeing with Rosenfeld that most Americans had never allowed a real contact to exist between them and their country, that America had been born old, and needed to find roots to attain the vigor of youth, Williams set out to determine where and when the first contacts between America and the Americans should have taken place, and to plant his own roots where the original Americans had neglected to do so, for "unless everything that is proclaimed a ground on which it stand, it has no worth."[14] Some of the results of his explorations were first published in *Broom* during 1923. The book itself appeared in 1925. Moving through history to pinpoint the reason why the American never established roots, he focused on the attitude of the Puritans. "If the 'puritan' in them," he argued, "could have ended with

[12] *Ibid.*, 335.

[13] *Autobiography*, 178.

[14] William Carlos Williams, *In the American Grain* (1925), paperback reprint (New York 1956), 109. Subsequent page references in the text are to this edition.

their entry into the New World and the subtle changes of growth at once started ... everything would have been different" (67), but instead of taking to the earth they sought after "a terrifying unknown image"; instead of responding to the truth their senses could have found around them, they based their existence on the "other-where" of their religion. Thus they "befouled" the New World. "All that they saw they lived by but denied" (112). "The Puritan, finding one thing like another in a world destined for blossom only in 'Eternity,' all soul, all 'emptiness' then here, was precluded from SEEING the Indian. They never realized the Indian in the least save as an unformed PURITAN" (113).

The attitude which developed among the Americans as a result of this influence was one of blindness to the world around them. Men like Franklin used their energy "to the smaller, narrower, protective thing and not to the great, New World" (157). They smudged the purity of what they touched, using everything for "practical" reasons only. They used science to create the money-making machine, not to discover the beauty of the objective world. Machines were a means to escape the fearful reality of the objective world, fearful because fraught with emotional uncertainty. "Machines were not so much to save time as to save dignity that fears the animate touch. It is miraculous the energy that goes into inventions here." This energy had its origin in "fear that robs the emotions; a mechanism to increase the gap between touch and thing, *not* to have a contact" (177). "The impact of the bare soul upon the very twist of the fact which is our world about us, is un-American. *That* we shun and rush off to the laboratory." As a result "our life is tortuous and grotesque, huge fetishes by which we are ruled in utter darkness—or we fly abroad for sensation: anything to escape—we fear simplicity as the plague. NEVER to allow touch" (178).

The origin of the American subterfuge, the American lack of indigenous experience, was seen by Williams in terms nearly identical to those of Rosenfeld. He, like Rosenfeld, saw the only solution for the contemporary American in search of roots in an intense effort to "touch" the facts of the objective reality around him, to establish a contact with his immediate environment. For Williams the perfect example of a man who had succeeded in doing this was Père Sébastian Rasles. "For everything his fine sense, blossoming, thriving, opening, reviving—not shutting out—was tuned." This was ultimately what it took: "to create, to hybridize, to cross-pollenize," instead of drawing back, instead of hiding in otherwheres (121). It meant exposing oneself, as Rosenfeld had said, to the sun.

Rosenfeld had argued that although Albert P. Ryder was the first American painter to establish contact with his environment, he did so imperfectly and was still "a blinded man in the moon," who could look at reality only with the soft focus of sundown. He pointed out that Ryder's imperfect grasp of reality showed itself in a very peculiar way in his paintings. The paintings of the great European masters are "convex at the very base of the canvas, commence swelling with forms of large amount in their foreground," which continue throughout the painting. Thus "the portion of the canvas which is most directly related to the abdominal centres of the human being, the foreground, was made as rich and expressive as any of the painting." For these men, Rosenfeld said, there was no necessity "to 'flee' from the foreground of life, and consequently from the present moment, into the past and the future. But in the Ryders, which stem from the undeveloped sensuality of the gilded age, the velvet-black and brown canvases become convex with form only in the centre of the canvases. Almost never do they commence their swell at the lower edge of the picture. The lower edge of your Ryder, indeed, is almost sure to be an evasion, a space hidden in darkness, passed over."[15] Yet if Ryder was the sundown, Rosenfeld added,

"then Arthur B. Davies is pale green moonlight. This painter has exquisite taste, poetical feeling, daintiness. He has, it would seem, as sensitive a response to the work of the artists of his own and other times, as any American painter, Max Weber alone, perhaps, excepted. But there is no virility in the man's own art. Davies' paintings seem like pages out of the life of a dreamy and wealthy spinster. One feels that a young girl, or an old young girl might have composed his charming fantasies, his tender and wan harmonies, but not a man. It is all so virginal, so charming and decorative, so safely guarded against virile passion and virile procreativeness. Davies appears to paint nude women; but there is no woman in his paint. The flesh of his superhuman figures has the quality of candy. One knows that, were one to touch these breasts with the lips, they would taste sickishly of pink taffy. It is for this reason that Davies is the painter preferred of the American women. For the woman who fears her own sexuality, and hates the male who appeals directly to it, finds in the art of Arthur B. Davies the man she wants men to be. Here, all is tender, dreamy, poeticized, sterilized, sentimentalized."[16]

Williams adapted these remarks and used them to show how the American artist's aesthetic reflected the position of women in American society. What Williams says has all the compression of his own unmistakable

[15] Rosenfeld, "American Painting," 652.
[16] *Ibid.*, 656.

style, but it is equally clear that Rosenfeld was the source of his remarks: "The aesthetic shown by American artists (the test of the women) is discouraging: the New England eunuchs,—'no more sex than a tapeworm' —faint echoes of England, perhaps of France, of Rousseau, as Valéry Larbaud insists,—Rider [sic]: no detail in his foregrounds just remote lusts, fiery but 'gone,'— Poe: moonlight. It is the annunciation of the spiritual barrenness of the American woman" (181).

Williams regarded Edgar Allan Poe as the first truly American poet for very much the same reasons that the Stieglitz group regarded Ryder as the first "American" painter. Poe, he said, was the first to speak for the modern poets, for "it is the New World, or to leave that for the better term, it is a *new locality* that is in Poe assertive; it is America, the first great burst through to expression of a re-awakening genius of place" (216), and therefore "what he says, being thoroughly local in origin, has some chance of being universal in application, a thing [others] never dared conceive. Made to fit a *place* it will have that actual quality of *things* anti-metaphysical" (222).

Considering the position Williams took in *In the American Grain*, it should have been no surprise to him that it caught Stieglitz's fancy; in fact, had Stieglitz rejected Williams' position he would have been in the unlikely position of rejecting his own ideas. The evenings Williams spent at Stieglitz's rooms, and his acquaintance with Hartley and Rosenfeld, had clearly had their effect. It is therefore rather disingenuous of Williams to have tried to obscure the fact that he had been closely connected with the Stieglitz group in the years before the appearance of *In the American Grain*. After all, as he himself remarked, in pointing out that Hart Crane used one of the chapters of his book in *The Bridge*: "He took what he wanted, why shouldn't he—that's what writing is for."[17] Moreover, *In the American Grain*, even if not original in its theories, remains one of Williams' major achievements, for, as Williams used to remark, "it is not what you say but the manner in which you say it," that ultimately counts for the artist.[18]

Williams continued to have close associations with the Stieglitz group during the remainder of the Twenties and throughout the Thirties, and his essays about the role of the poet throughout the rest of his life show that Stieglitz's attitudes had a lasting effect on him. They gave a structural justification for the poetry he wanted to write, and they gave him a theoretical basis from which he could approach the work of others. Thus when in the late Twenties he came to write about Gertrude Stein, he could emphasize with confidence that "to be democratic, local (in the sense of being attached with integrity to actual experience), Stein, or any other artist, must for subtlety ascend to a plane of almost abstract design to keep alive. To writing, then, as an art in itself. Yet what actually impinges on the senses must be rendered as it appears, by the use of which, only, and under which, untouched, the significance has to be disclosed."[19] And in discussing Marianne Moore he could rejoice in the fact that for her "an apple remains an apple whether it be in Eden or the fruitbowl where it curls."[20] When in 1939 he published his "Study of the Artist," he could affirm that for the artist "the only world that exists is the world of the senses," and that "if I succeed in keeping myself objective enough, sensual enough, I can produce the factors, the concretions of materials by which others shall understand and so be led to use—that they

[17] *I Wanted To Write a Poem*, 43.
[18] *Selected Essays*, xii.
[19] *Ibid.*, 118.
[20] *Ibid.*, 125.

139

may better see, touch, taste, enjoy—their own world *differing as it may* from mine."[21] Talking about the work of his friend Charles Sheeler, finally, he could say, "for the artist, for Sheeler as an artist, it is in the shape of the thing that the essence lies."[22]

Williams' espousal of the concept of the "thing itself," as being the basis for all truly contemporary expression, had all-important implications for the subject matter of his poems, but it also had a significant influence on his approach to the question of the structure of the poem itself. If objects are the only things that matter to the artist, he argued, then the poem as poem should matter to him as well, for the poem is ultimately also an object. As an object it has a right to be regarded as an autonomous thing, and to be studied "in terms of its own shapes and volumes." The arrangement of words on a page therefore takes on as much importance for the poet as the careful arrangement of natural forms and structures on a canvas for a painter. The poet's words, indeed, are not only his pigment, but also the natural forms and structures of the poem as object. Williams' first statement of this attitude came, appropriately, in *Spring and All.* Here he argued, in fact, that each word should be seen as an object in itself which, just like the objects in the material world, is being used by the majority of people without any regard for its intrinsic meaning. The poet, therefore, should "re-valuate" the words he uses, just as he takes the objects of the real world and makes them take on their clearest significance by isolating them in such a fashion that they are seen in the way he wishes them to be seen. He should "liberate" the words in a similar fashion, and by removing them from the "fixities which destroy" them, remove them from extraneous

[21] *Ibid.,* 197.
[22] *Ibid.,* 233.

implications until they once more become "accurately tuned" to the facts which give them their own objective reality.[23] Presumably, although Williams does not specifically say so in *Spring and All*, the poet can achieve this re-valuation of the words he uses by carefully arranging their position in his poem so that their "bloom" will be restored by the unusual emphasis they receive, much as a Cubist painter such as Juan Gris will carefully arrange the objects in his painting in such a fashion that their unusual conjunction makes us more clearly aware of their individual significance as objects.

During the Twenties Williams did not pursue the theoretical implications of this concept of poetic structure very actively, but it is clear that it was the basis for his formulation of the theory of Objectivism in the early Thirties, which saw the poem as an autonomous object with an intrinsic structural necessity removed from the tyranny of rhyme, conventional rhythm, and metaphor, and constructed solely out of words representing real things. Or, as Williams at the time said in an essay on Pound, "the word has been used in its plain sense to represent a thing—remaining thus loose in its context—not gummy—(when at its best)—an objective unit in the design—but alive."[24] In his introduction to *The Wedge* he elaborated: "When a man makes a poem, makes it, mind you, he takes words as he finds them interrelated about him and composes them—without distortion which would mar their exact significances—into an intense expression of his perceptions and ardors that they may constitute a revelation in the speech that he uses. It isn't what he says that counts as a work of art, it's what he makes, with such intensity of perception that it

[23] *Spring and All*, 93.
[24] *Selected Essays*, 110.

lives with an intrinsic movement of its own to verify its authenticity."[25]

Although Williams' poetry for the greater part of his career was not determined in its structure by anything but the immediate visual object, he was pursued by what he considered the inescapable conclusion that a poem is like the canvas of a painting, and that words in a poem serve as the visual objects which, like the paint on a canvas, have to be arranged in the manner most appropriate to a faithful representation of the aspect of the objective world constituting the material for the poem. In the Forties and Fifties this consideration drove him to hunt with singular tenacity for what he called an appropriate "measure," and led him to his final structural discovery: the "variable foot."

Stieglitz and his followers, then, had a strong influence on Williams' theory of the function of the artist and on his ideas concerning the proper materials for art. Williams was very well aware of his indebtedness to Stieglitz and knew that his concept of the local as the basis for true universality in art, and his belief in the creative moment expressed through the materials of the concrete world had been given their focus by the pronouncements of the photographer and the attitudes of the members in the group around him. Even as late as 1943 he sent Stieglitz a group of aphorisms having to do with the concept of place, appending a note saying: "Haven't seen you recently but thought you might be interested."[26] The "axioms," as he called them, reiterated the need for the artist to be always aware that "place is the only universal." It is, however, in his essay "The American Background," which opened the volume of tributes to

[25] *Ibid.*, 257.

[26] Unpublished letter to Stieglitz, July 17, 1943, Stieglitz Archive, Yale.

Stieglitz published in 1934, that Williams is most specific about the photographer's significance to American culture. It was only appropriate that the author of *In the American Grain* should here once more cover the elements of American history, in language familiar to all who were acquainted with Stieglitz and his work. Again Williams defined the concept of place as underlying any significant move towards a national identity. What, he asked, is culture, but "the realization of the qualities of a place in relation to the life which occupies it; embracing everything involved, climate, geographic position, relative size, history, other cultures—as well as the character of its sands, flowers, minerals, and the condition of knowledge within its borders. It is the act of lifting these things to an ordered and utilized whole, which is culture. . . . The act is the thing."[27] And because this is true, American painting—and Williams might have added, American poetry as well—must be "related to its own definite tradition, its own environment and general history," just as much as French painting is. This is exactly what Stieglitz set out to do: "Realizing the fullness and color in French painting—certainly one of the delights of the modern world—he went directly to work, a real act of praise, by striving to push forward something that would be or that was comparable in America." Through his own art, photography, Stieglitz set the example:

"The photographic camera and what it could do were particularly well suited to a place where the immediate and the actual were under official neglect. Stieglitz inaugurated an era based solidly on a correct understanding of the cultural relationships; but the difficulties he encountered both from within and without were colossal. He fought them clear-sightedly.

[27] *America and Alfred Stieglitz*, 29.

143

"The effect of his life and work has been to bend together and fuse, against whatever resistance, the split forces of the two necessary cultural groups: (1) the local effort, well understood in defined detail and (2) the forces from the outside."[28]

To combine "the local effort" with the stylistic innovations, "the forces from the outside," which he had taken from the European avant garde painters, is of course exactly what Williams set out to do as the 1910's came to a close. And in the photography of Stieglitz, in the paintings of Sheeler, Marin, Hartley, and Demuth, he found his appropriate texts.

[28] *Ibid.*, 31-32.

VI. THE HIEROGLYPHICS OF A NEW SPEECH

*W*HEN STIEGLITZ began to exhibit the work of European artists at 291, he did so because he recognized that their interest in the autonomous significance of the materials of the objective world was similar to his own. He realized that he could teach the American artists how to truly *see* a thing in terms of its volumes, outlines, and planes, by pointing to the details of Cézanne's, and later Picasso's, analysis of the visual and tactile properties which constitute an object. Stieglitz, of course, had long ago made the discovery that the spatial and structural relationships between objects, their textures and their forms, when emphasized properly and removed as much as possible from an extraneous, contextual environment, can come to represent in their freedom from anecdotal reference, experiences which touch upon the most profound pre-rational, and therefore otherwise indefinable emotional sources of man's actions. The qualities in Stieglitz's prints were similar to those emphasized by the new painting, and it is therefore altogether appropriate that his photograph "The Steerage," made in 1907, the year of "Les Demoiselles d'Avignon," should have elicited Picasso's admiring approval. Picasso is reported to have remarked that Stieglitz was "working in the same spirit as he."[1] In *The Egoist*, in fact, Huntley Carter commented: "One can imagine a Cézanne abstraction putting tracing paper on 'The Steerage' and abstracting the woman seated in a deeply reflective attitude as representing the sum of human interest in the scene, or a Picassonian abstracting the gangway and the

[1] See unpublished letter from Marius de Zayas to Stieglitz, June 11, 1914, Stieglitz Archive, Yale; and Alfred Stieglitz, "Four Happenings," *Twice a Year*, viii-ix (Fall-Winter 1942), 134.

steerage ladder, with their fine composition of straights and curves, as providing the essential signature of the scene."[2]

Toward 1915, however, while the painters of the Stieglitz group were still trying to determine how they might best take account of the implications of Cubism, the European painters began more and more to emphasize a kind of "pure abstraction." They began to talk about the "tyranny" of the object, and wanted to do away with the object as seen in the material world, or they began to play games with it rather than try to establish "contact."[3] Stieglitz felt that intellectualism was beginning to dominate their approach even more rigidly than before, and he deplored this development. He considered intellectualism ultimately a hindrance to the artist who wished to express the essence of things. He began more and more to disassociate himself from these aspects of modern art. Abstraction, he believed, should at most serve as a means, never as an end. The Europeans, who implicitly understood their relationship to the objects of the material world, could perhaps afford to be playful, but the American artists had only recently discovered the real world. They had only just begun to understand that they should go, as Marin said, "to the elemental big forms" and to the "relatively little things that grow on the mountain's back. Which if you don't recognize you don't recognize the mountain."[4] America was to be affirmed through a clear definition of its material proper-

[2] Huntley Carter, "Two Ninety One," *The Egoist*, III, 3 (March 1916).

[3] See pages 79-80 above.

[4] Quoted by Frederick S. Wight, "John Marin—Frontiersman," in M, the Catalogue of the John Marin Memorial Exhibition, University of California Art Galleries, Los Angeles, 1955.

ties, and if abstraction was to be used it should constitute a means by which the artist uncovered the essential lines and volumes of the American object. The American artist's initial concern should be to isolate properties of line existing in concrete materials. He should furthermore eliminate those materials not necessary, or indeed obstructive, to a clear vision of the object's most salient forms. As Arthur Dove wrote in 1914: "One *means* used at ' 291 ' has been a process of elimination of the non-essential."[5]

In his photography, Stieglitz gave an important indication of how the American artist could use the principles of abstraction and simplification to his advantage without abandoning his search for a meaningful expression of his environment. In a series of prints entitled "From the Window—'291,'" which he made in 1915, he recorded aspects of New York City in night and snow. One of these shows the top of a tree, its barren twigs heavy with new snow, jutting out against the grey-black walls of the buildings surrounding it. While unmistakably a tree, the edges of the black, gnarled twigs against the whiteness of the snow and the whiteness of the snow-covered twigs against the grim dark background, combine to form the abstract patterns of a frenetic dance without warmth, of silence without rest, a tree caught in the rhythm of a city which does not accept the meaning of the seasons it is forced to endure.

Another of the prints in this series shows the city at night, the diagonal planes of rooftops receding into the verticals of ever higher buildings, the darkness of the foreground cut in triangular patterns by the outlines of the flat roofs, lit up faintly by the weak light falling on their snow-covered edges. The central horizontal plane

[5] Arthur Dove in "What Is 291?" *Camera Work*, 47 (July 1914).

of the picture is broken sharply by hard electric lights which carve out the vertical rectangles of a window and a door. These rectangles find dazzling rows of echoes in the towering buildings of the upper distance. The rhythm of sharp, angular planes is broken in the foreground by the shallow curve of a line of washing. Although it is a picture of night, the electric light gives it an air of cold and lonely expectancy. The bright, but mist-suffused rectangles of the foreground windows, isolated from the many uniform rows of rectangles lighting up the buildings in the background, become expressive of the human "one" isolated from the "many" in the ever-more-indifferent stone patterns of city existence. The forms are quite Cubist: space is abstracted and broken into visual planes, the outlines of the roofs have the same linear, angular movement found in the spatial constructions of Cubism. But the origin of the materials has not been obscured. Ultimately we know that these are the lines, planes, and volumes of a city, and that together they are the city. In the end it is the city we see revealing one aspect of its meaning through itself (Plate xi).

But the visual space of these prints was still quite complex, perhaps due to the unwieldy size of "the city" as object. Stieglitz now began more and more to find "equivalents" to his feelings in smaller objects, or parts of objects. The object could be a woman, a barn, a tree, or grass. During the later 1910's he made many remarkable portraits, especially of Georgia O'Keeffe, one of these consisting solely of a closeup of her hands, posed gracefully, fan-like between the sharp curves of her breasts. The portrait becomes an abstract pattern of lines, qualities of light, and tactile values, but meaningful primarily because it is part of reality, part of life, part of the organic significance of all feminine qualities in the objective world. Beyond that, the print reveals certain elements of the individual character of Georgia O'Keeffe, and is therefore a portrait in the most specific sense of the word.

In other prints Stieglitz focused closely on the sides or the gables of old wooden barns at Lake George, their shingles and boards and the texture of wood becoming the sole materials for his picture. Or, moving his lens close to the trees, he caught the rhythm of dance in their knotted branches and the strangely tense, nervous quality of birch bark suffused with light (Plate xii). He photographed with needle-sharp focus a thin branch weighted down with heavy apples, wet with raindrops against a bright, jagged pattern of shingles and a pointed gable, or a single apple, glistening with rain, surrounded by leaves (Plate x). As Jean Toomer wrote, through pictures such as these Stieglitz made people realize "the treeness of a tree . . . what bark is. . . . Here in these prints our earth is as it *is*, our dwellings are as they *are*, ourselves, we humans, as we *are*."[6] These were the materials of objective reality, expressed in their own terms and thus shown to be representative in form and line, in light and texture, of all the emotions of which man is capable. Stieglitz was afraid of no aspect of reality, recorded the most intensely erotic as well as the most purely ascetic. He photographed, with unflinching sharpness and immediacy, a woman's torso, partly in water, her pubic hair black against a shimmering belly, her breasts very full and heavy, her skin cold and wet, her nipples hard. He photographed clouds in purely abstract patterns of black and white, or a branch, stripped of its leaves and bark, reaching up tortuously into an empty sky. The lines between earth and sky were endlessly expressive to him. He once said to Dorothy Norman that

[6] Jean Toomer, "The Hill," in *America and Alfred Stieglitz*, 299.

"if he could really put down the line of the mountain and sky as they touch, as he [had] seen it across Lake George from his house on the Hill, it would include all of life"[7] (Plate XIII).

The painters of 291 followed Stieglitz closely in his move towards simplification. After a short flirtation with Cubism in the style of Picasso they concerned themselves more and more specifically with the precise delineation of the American object. Toward 1917 all had abandoned the search for abstract form and were beginning to define the content of their paintings purely in terms of the materials found in the real world. Hartley was originally influenced by the work of Kandinsky and the German expressionists, and went through a period in 1914 and 1915 in which he abstracted in bright yellows, reds, and blacks the elements of German army life, although these "abstractions" were still closely bound to specific objects: the iron crosses, standards, and epaulettes of the military are solidly presented. The closest Hartley came to real abstraction was in such paintings as his 1916 "Movement Nr. Nine," which consists of large planes of solid color fitted together like wedges on a board. But his "Movement Nr. Ten" of 1917 brings us back to recognizable objects: bananas and a pear on a plate, solid shapes presented through their most essential qualities of line and color. After that, Hartley concentrated on establishing a meaningful fusion between the universal qualities inherent in the volumes and colors of things, and their appearance. He reduced the lines of clouds, mountains, bottles, trees, and rocks to their minimum, while emphasizing their real solidity through hard contrasts of bright color and a gritty emphasis on earthy textures and greyish-white tones. Thus, at its best, Hartley's work presents the objective world in terms of its

[7] *America and Alfred Stieglitz*, 135.

most basic tactile and visual qualities; even his clouds become in these pictures as solidly real as his rocks.

Arthur Dove took a step Hartley was never really capable of making: he moved to the very center of his materials. His colors are the pure textures of bark, soil, rock, and plant, transposed directly onto his canvas. His paintings come closer to pure abstraction than those of the others in the Stieglitz group. But it always remained Dove's purpose to distill the essentials of his organic environment through its textures, colors, and lines. He succeeded better than Hartley, because he found a way to use the actual shapes of nature, not stylized shapes based on nature as Hartley's too often were. In such a painting as his "A Walk Poplars" of 1920, he focuses closely on a tree's trunk and faithfully transposes the true linear rhythms of part of its shape onto his canvas (Plate XIV). During the early 1910's Dove had been painting natural forms in a stylized fashion closely akin to Hartley's later practice. These paintings were much less distinctive than the work he did from the close of that decade onward. The effect of those earlier paintings was diluted by their rigidity. Thus his painting "plantforms" of 1915 loses much of its effect because he presents these plant forms not in terms of their natural shapes, but stylized, reduced to patterns of straight lines and curves, whose origin was more intellectual, abstractionist, in the European sense, than based on a transposition onto canvas of actual shapes existing in nature. The same "intellectualism" reduces the sense of reality to be found in such a painting as "Sails" of 1911, which is even more obviously based on Cubist and Futurist ideas. There is solidity and a sense of concrete materials in these paintings but it is an objectivism which finds its origin and justification in the intellect rather than in the object itself. Once Dove had rid himself of his tendency towards

151

intellectualism and had called himself "back to the simple feeling for life," he was able to "feel the 'live line,' which stimulates life in the observer."[8] After that he could say with ease that "there is no such thing as abstraction, it is extraction"; no matter how abstract his compositions may seem at first sight, closer examination will always bring us straight to the rocks, the soil, the leaves, barns, telegraph poles and wires, boat wrecks, moons, industrial tanks, caverns, bridges, coal-carriers, and even popsicles from which he drew his colors, shapes, and textures. As Frederick Wight has remarked: "In Dove's painting nature is like the pattern in polished marble: the pattern is altogether natural, yet not to be found until man has cut a plane through the rock."[9] During the 1920's Dove became so anxious to capture all the qualities of his materials in perfect accuracy in his paintings that he began to incorporate actual pieces of wood, wire and cloth, in his compositions, thus bringing "organic function" to a practice he undoubtedly took from the Dadaists (Plate xv).

Dove was virtually the only artist other than Stieglitz whose work Georgia O'Keeffe really admired. In many ways her painting represents a synthesis of the textural and linear accuracy of Stieglitz, and of Dove's practice of extracting the essential visual qualities from the things around him. Following the indication given by Stieglitz's photography that even the structure of parts of objects can represent fully the universal and autonomous significance of the object as a whole, she set herself to observing plant forms with minute accuracy, expressing in terms of subtle contrasts of color suffused with bright light the shapes of parts of flowers microscopically seen,

[8] Quoted in Frederick Wight, *Arthur G. Dove* (Berkeley 1958), 37.
[9] *Ibid.*

152

enlarged into gigantic shapes (Plate xvi). By deleting all extraneous or secondary forms she created through color and line a world made tangible and visible in its purely distilled function as source of our most intense feelings. "I found that I could say things with color and shapes that I couldn't say in any other way—things that I had no words for."[10] In one of his many portraits of her, Stieglitz has caught her bent over a tiny flower, transplanting the lines made by its petals onto the field of a huge canvas. Under her scrutiny plants, while never losing their identity, became as folds of skin or phallic shapes expressive of much more than simply human sexuality. White skulls, rocks, or hills became parts of a man's or a woman's body, balanced between dark and light, the visual equivalents to man's subconscious sources of action.

It would seem clear that O'Keeffe's pervasive use of sharply etched line finds its origin in Stieglitz's photography. The photographers before Stieglitz had shied away from sharply focused images; they wanted to approximate the ethereal qualities which soft, complementary colors and the use of imaginary and conflicting sources of diffused light usually give to even the most naturalistic paintings. By resolutely breaking through the photographers' fear of sharp outlines, Stieglitz emphasized, especially in his work of the 1910's and 1920's, an aspect of the relationship between line and light which was at that time still largely ignored in the visual arts. Elements of this relationship had been detected by Ingres and other realists of the nineteenth century, but had been obscured by the development of Impressionism. Stieglitz took the world and fixed the three-dimensional qualities of things in the two-dimensional field of pho-

[10] Quoted in Daniel Catton Rich, *Georgia O'Keeffe* (Chicago 1943), 7.

tography. His prints showed, far more directly than had ever been the case before, that to the eye direct vision of an object is determined by means of lines of needle-thin, absolute sharpness, that the lines of reality have all the precision of the finest lines of an etching. The photographs further showed that these lines were most clearly defined when used to divide different qualities of brightness and shade or, in painting, brighter or more subdued colors. They also showed that line loses its sharpness when used to divide strongly contrasting color values, unless the contrasting tonalities are modified and subdued at the line of touch. Stieglitz's photographs, in other words, defined how daylight, and especially sunlight, is seen in two-dimensional terms; that in most cases shade is actually contained in visual planes of uniform tonality, bounded by sharp linear divisions determined in form and intensity by the volume of the object on which it depends, and that shade does not usually merely dissolve in fuzzy intergranulation with the objects over which it falls.

One of the best examples of the direct application to painting of these visual rules discovered by photography can be found in Charles Sheeler's "Bucks County Barns" (1923), now at the Whitney Museum in New York. The outlines of these sun-drenched barns are razor-sharp, and so are the planes of shade thrown by gables and shadow sides, creating an intricate rhythm of finely etched geometric shapes, without ever obscuring the totality of the barns as barns (Plate xvii). Sheeler, of course, was also an outstanding photographer, whose original indebtedness to his older contemporary has been established. He frequently both painted and photographed the materials under his scrutiny, and of all the painters associated with Stieglitz, his work became perhaps most directly analogous to photography. Yet as

154

late as 1915 his painting had been quite "abstract" and Cubist in orientation, consisting of roughly outlined shapes and deliberately sketchy brushwork. As the Stieglitz group veered away from Europe, Sheeler followed, and his work became more and more concerned with the precise delineation of form. Like O'Keeffe, he began to adapt the sharply etched outlines of light and shade which photography had taught him to recognize, into the equivalent value of tone and color in painting. Thus he expressed his contact with the materials of his environment in purely objective terms. He expressed his fascination for the industrial and architectural shapes of America by emphasizing in his painting the solidity and classic purity these monumental shapes can assume when seen through the linear definition of camera tones (Plate xviii). But although Sheeler abandoned Cubism as such, his work continued to evince its structural influence, particularly in his use of "force lines" to anchor and to solidify his compositions. These force lines were frequently continuations of the outlines of objects which had been painted accurately but which were now pulled into a certain direction by these lines, and thereby made to continue beyond their actual shapes. Thus the force lines could be used to mark the division between two tones of color in, for instance, the sky. In this fashion Sheeler created an effect analogous to the spatial fragmentation practiced by the Cubists, and this gave an added sense of solidity to his compositions in general. A good example of this practice can be found in his "Pertaining to Yachts and Yachting" (1922), now at the Philadelphia Museum of Art.

Charles Demuth used "force lines" similar to those of Sheeler, and indeed used them more often and more effectively. Sheeler's work tends toward monumentality and hard, pure color, while Demuth emphasized more subtle relationships between man and the material world, using watercolor almost exclusively as his medium. He was one of the first among the painters in the Stieglitz group to discover 291, and was visiting it as early as 1908. His work at that time was quite undistinguished, although it showed a preoccupation with line. During the early 1910's Demuth spent much of his time illustrating episodes from works by writers such as Zola and Henry James. By 1917 he had developed the use of sharp, thin outlines. Combining his use of clear, precise line with the force lines and planar structure he took from Cubism, he developed a style which was quite literally a fusion of photographic and Cubist qualities. A good example of this fusion is his painting "Machinery" (1920), which expresses shade in terms very similar to Sheeler's "Bucks County Barns"—solid tonal qualities with hard edges. As a result, the metal of the pipes and machinery takes on a steely illumination which brings us directly to tactile and visual reality. Thus the Cubist compression of the focal center of the painting intensifies our awareness of the objects in it, and forces us to evaluate the contrast between the sensuous curves of the machinery and the austere straight linear patterns of the windows behind it (Plate xix).

Whenever Demuth portrayed an aspect of industrial life or of the city—themes, in other words, which required the expression of elements of tension—whenever he felt the influence of what Marin called "pull forces," he would express them through force lines, slashing incisions of fields of tonal variety whose intensity increased the more he felt the tension inherent in the objects he wished to depict. But whenever he focused on the objects of nature—fruits, flowers, plants—he centered them on his paper, giving their shapes full attention and recording them with a lucid veracity and subtlety of tone which extended the use of linear precision beyond even the power of photography. For Demuth could freely choose which elements to bring out, which lines to delete, and which to emphasize. In these pictures often a single line suffices to indicate shade. They are representative of nature perceived in its fullest visual intensity. A good example of this aspect of Demuth at his best can be found in his watercolor "Green Pears" (1929) in the Yale University Art Gallery.

John Marin was closest to Stieglitz in age and in many ways his bond with Stieglitz was closest too. He was the first of the painters at 291 to reach artistic maturity. In a credo for his annual exhibition at 291, in 1912, he stated the essence of his style; what he said about his watercolors of New York City, which were doubtless inspired largely by Stieglitz's relentless photographic explorations of the city, was representative of the photographer's beliefs as much as of his own, as is evident from the lengthy quotations Stieglitz took from it for his article on the upcoming Armory Show for the Sunday *New York American*. Marin asked:

"Shall we consider the life of a great city as confined simply to the people and animals on its streets and in its buildings? Are the buildings themselves dead? We have been told somewhere that a work of art is a thing alive. You cannot create a work of art unless the things you behold respond to something within you. Therefore if these buildings move me they too must have life. Thus the whole city is alive; buildings, people, all are alive; and the more they move me the more I feel them to be alive. It is this 'moving of me' that I try to express, so that I may recall the spell I have been under and behold the expression of the different emotions that have been called into being. . . .

"I see great forces at work; great movements; the large

157

buildings and the small buildings; the warring of the great and the small; influences of one mass on another greater or smaller mass. Feelings are aroused which give me the desire to express the reaction of these 'pull forces,' those influences which play with one another; great masses pulling smaller masses, each subject in some degree to the other's power.

"And so," Marin concluded, "I try to express graphically what a great city is doing."[11] He followed the same procedure in his explorations of the Maine coast and hills, New Mexico and the sea. In each case he expressed the essentials of what he saw in quick watercolors, in which real, but barely visible phenomena such as sky, clouds, the wind, were represented in washes, jagged lines, or blocked planes, the force lines and the "warring, pushing, pulling forces" he saw in the objective world. As a result, his work became a visual script, recording the world through the universal qualities of color, shape, texture, and light. The fewer the obstructing elements, the better; simplification, one line in place of many, was the key to an accurate record of experience. "Painting is like golf," Marin once said, "the fewer strokes I can take, the better the picture."[12] In a letter to Stieglitz he wrote: "When a man loves material and will not under any circumstances destroy its own inherent beauty, then and then only can that wonderful thing we call art be created."[13] He scoffed at those who declared that they did not "paint rocks, trees, houses and all other things seen," but an "inner vision." This was rubbish, he said: "If you have an intense love and feeling toward these

[11] John Marin on his New York Sequences, 1912, exhibition statement reprinted in *Camera Work*, 42-43 (April-July 1913), 18.
[12] Quoted in MacKinley Helm, *John Marin* (New York 1948), 37.
[13] *Ibid.*, 96.

things, you'll try your damndest to put on paper, on canvas, that thing. You can transpose, you can play with and on your material, but when you are finished that's got to have the roots of that thing in it and no other thing."[14] Any "vision," any meaning an artist conveys in his work, must be inherent in the thing itself.

Consequently the artists in the Stieglitz group, to "re-true" themselves, to establish their contact with their environment, with their "moment," went back "from time to time to the elemental big forms—Sky, Sea, Mountain, Plain," as Marin said,[15] and to all the objects which constitute reality: to buildings, grass, barns, earth, skyscrapers, factory chimneys, trees, machinery, the city skyline and the line between sky and mountain, rocks and flowers, cars, locomotives, and cows. There was only one object that scarcely appeared in relationship to other objects in their pictures: Man. Stieglitz made portraits, it is true, but those represented man as object, as *ding an sich*, or as part of a natural unit of man and thing: a hand on the hubcap of a car. Of the painters, Marin occasionally included human figures; clowns in a circus, women-forms and sea; and Demuth's early book illustrations and studies of vaudeville naturally contained human forms. But the others, as much as Demuth in his later work, ignored man almost entirely because to include man would detract from the object expressed; man's obsession with man tends to obliterate the right of the object to be seen; when man and object are put together, the object loses its autonomy and becomes metaphor, and man becomes anecdote.

As has been shown, the intentions of the artists discussed here were similar throughout their association

[14] *Ibid.*
[15] Quoted in Frederick S. Wight, "John Marin—Frontiersman," *op.cit.*

with Stieglitz: "to show the moment to itself," to speak of life through the materials of the real world. That Stieglitz was their taskmaster in this search for expression was beyond doubt. As Georgia O'Keeffe said, "he was the leader or he didn't play. It was his game and we all played along or left the game."[16]

Yet in the disparate methods these artists chose, they expressed their individuality. Their skill in adapting to the possibilities of expression offered to them in the liberating creative atmosphere which dominated the progressive artistic circles of New York during the 1910's is the key to the excellence of their work. Together they emphasized in a serious effort, for the first time in the history of American culture, a truly American way of looking at things; together they created what Egmont Arens called, in reference to Stieglitz's photographs, "the hieroglyphics of a new speech between those of us who find all the spoken languages too clumsy."[17] Had it not been for Stieglitz's relentless advocacy of this new speech, and the articulate exposition of the meaning of its hieroglyphics by Paul Rosenfeld and others, its significance and implications might have been lost to those who were only loosely associated with the movement. The importance of these hieroglyphics extended beyond the realm of painting. To William Carlos Williams it seemed that poetry could make use of them too; attuned as he was to visual experience, it was not surprising that he set out to adapt them to his own purpose.

[16] Georgia O'Keeffe, "Stieglitz: His Pictures Collected Him," *New York Times Magazine* (December 11, 1949), 24.

[17] Egmont Arens, "Alfred Stieglitz: His Cloud Pictures," *Playboy*, 9 (July 1924), 15.

VII. THE POEM AS STILL-LIFE

KORA IN HELL marked Williams' most protracted experiment with image fragmentation, at least for the time being. It did not take long before he became dissatisfied with the results of that book. He had "always had a feeling of identity with nature,"[1] and he began to realize that abstraction, if it became other than the process of "extraction" Arthur Dove had referred to, could easily obliterate nature rather than celebrate it. He now saw that, although the Improvisations had taught him a way to "revalue experience," he had, in writing them, let himself go too far from the objects of experience. He had taken "recourse to the expedient of letting life go completely," and this had resulted in a "dislocation of sense" which was opposed to the aims of his poetry.[2] For "the exaltation men feel before a work of art is the feeling of reality they draw from it," and therefore it should be "transfused with the same forces which transfuse the earth."[3] Consequently he began to adapt his poetry to the visual example of painters like Demuth and Hartley, realizing that his interests were more closely allied to their work than to the intellectualism of the European artists. At the same time he continued to adapt to his own uses stylistic elements of new Parisian art movements as they came along.

The element in Demuth's fragile watercolors of flowers Williams most admired was the singular immediacy of their focus, due to the painter's close observation of the organic forms and his careful selection of their most significant features. There was nothing vague about his

[1] *I Wanted To Write a Poem*, 21.
[2] *Spring and All*, 42-44.
[3] *Ibid.*, 61, 49.

treatment of the object. In studying Demuth's work, and that of the others in the Stieglitz group, Williams was beginning to realize that, as he was to say in *The Descent of Winter*, "in almost all verse you read, mine or anybody's else, the figures used and the general impression of the things spoken of is vague 'you could say it better in prose' especially good prose, say the prose of Hemingway. The truth of the object is somehow hazed over, dulled. . . . There is too often no observation in it, in poetry."[4] He therefore set out to approximate the features of Demuth's work in some of the poems of *Sour Grapes* (1921). Later he was to remark that he had used "straight observation . . . in four poems about flowers: 'Daisy,' 'Primrose' (this is the American primrose), 'Queen Anne's Lace,' and 'Great Mullen.' I thought of them as still lifes. I looked at the actual flowers as they grew."[5]

If we compare Williams' poem "Daisy" with a 1918 watercolor titled "Daisies" by Demuth, we can see how much the poet's method resembles the painter's style. Demuth, in his watercolor, makes the round, yellow-brown centers of the flowers his focal point. These spots are the first to hit our eyes, ringed as they are with circles of fragile white petals against a dark surface of leaves shot through with slender stems. Williams does essentially the same. In the first lines of his poem, by means of a quick play on the name of the flower, he calls the reader's attention to the visual significance of the flower's core:

> The dayseye hugging the earth
> in August, ha! Spring is
> gone down in purple . . .

[4] William Carlos Williams, "The Descent of Winter," *The Exile*, 1, 4 (Autumn 1928), 46.
[5] *I Wanted To Write a Poem*, 35.

Demuth, in his watercolor, after manipulating the focus of our initial impression of the flowers, continues to define in minute, but selective, detail, the features which contribute most to the further delineation of the daisies' singular attributes. We first notice the careless, uncultivated growth radiating outward from behind the flowers until that growth simply disappears in deliberately unfinished outlines toward the edge of the paper. Williams similarly defines the backdrop to the image of his daisy:

> weeds stand high in the corn,
> the rainbeaten furrow
> is clotted with sorrel
> and crabgrass, the
> branch is black under
> the heavy mass of the leaves—

Like Demuth's outline, Williams' delineation of the flower's surroundings remains deliberately unfinished at this point. Williams' subsequent description of the most important features of the daisy has a quality which is analogous to the visual qualities of the flower Demuth makes us notice on closer observation of his watercolor: the "slender green stem / ribbed lengthwise," the "yellow center, / split and creviced and done into / minute flowerheads," the "brownedged, / green and pointed scales," and finally the "crisp petals" which remain "brief, translucent, greenfastened, / barely touching at the edges." Demuth's razor-sharp, almost microscopically thin lines, and his careful, gauze-like treatment of the petals thus finds a series of very precise verbal analogues in the words of Williams' poem.

There is in Demuth's watercolor, however, a sense of unity which we do not yet get from Williams' attempt at still-life. Demuth, in his record of the flowers, limits himself to only their most salient features, thus forcing

us to attend to a very carefully selected assembly of
organic lines, revealing the essential qualities of the
daisy through selection and reduction of focus, as well
as through observation as such. Williams was at this
point not yet capable of such integrity of means. He fell
into the error of making his canvas too large, of adding
too many secondary objects which were essentially
extraneous to the central statement of his "still-life."
The poet, from Demuth's point of view, need not have
called our attention to the "rainbeaten furrow" or the
sorrel and crabgrass, and especially not to the branch,
"black under/ the heavy mass of the leaves," which
introduces an object that has a legitimate claim to being
studied as still-life in its own right, and in a poem of
its own. Williams, moreover fell into the trap which
throughout his career as a poet he attempted to but could
never entirely manage to avoid: the use of comparison,
of metaphor. By comparing the daisy to the sun, and
by comparing the petals to "blades of limpid seashell,"
he failed to adhere to his own intention of constructing
his "praise" of it so "as to borrow no particle from right
or left." He did not, as the Stieglitz group said he ought
to, and he earnestly wanted to, give "his poem over to
the flower and its plant themselves."[6] In this poem, therefore, Williams did create a still-life through the close
observation of a scene, and he did give his poem the
painterly qualities he was looking for, both in its conscious structure as a still-life, and in its absence of
narrative sequence and its broken pattern of visual
materials, but at the same time it has neither the dramatic, "Cubist," visual turmoil of such an earlier poem
as "Spring Strains" nor the clear immediate focus of a
Demuth. The poem's closest affinity is, in fact, still with

[6] See page 58.

the Improvisations—but, again, it does not have their swiftness, for it is too diffused.

Obviously Williams would have to diminish the "furniture" of his poems if he was to approximate the intense focus the Stieglitz group was looking for. He would have to give his poem over to the precise description of a single object within its immediate context, or to a close study of the direct interaction of two, or at least very few, equivalent objects. Williams' initial solution to the problem of how to achieve such a reduction and sharpening of focus was to limit the length of his poems, and to pair their brevity with a deceptively simple mode of observation which would carefully emphasize the one or two most salient features of the object under scrutiny. One of the earliest examples of this practice is "January Morning; Suite," from *Al Que Quiere*. Here Williams links fifteen very short poems, each containing one, or at most two, objects closely observed, to form a "suite" of essentially photographic images:

V

—and a young horse with a green bed-quilt
on his withers shaking his head:
bared teeth and nozzle high in the air!

VI

—and a semicircle of dirt-colored men
about a fire bursting from an old
ash can,

VII

—and the worn,
blue car rails (like the sky!)
gleaming among the cobbles!

In *Sour Grapes* Williams showed enough confidence in the legitimacy of this practice to allow such very short poems to stand on their own, and in some of these he managed to catch the structural precision of a Stieglitz photograph, an O'Keeffe, or a Demuth:

LINES
Leaves are grey green,
the grass broken, bright green.

By the time he saw the fire truck flashing past on his way to Hartley, he was able to combine the clear, objective selectivity which he saw in the work of his American friends with the concrete, "visible" language he had learned to use in his study of the Cubists. "The Great Figure" was, therefore, one of the first fruits of this propitious synthesis.

Williams, in following the Europeans, had already been writing poems whose meaning was contained in a single image, an image which was a careful enumeration of disparate materials that, brought together within the framework of the poem, formed a clearly delineated picture encompassing a wide range of visual experience: a simultaneous view of disparate elements of the world. Now, under the influence of the Stieglitz group, he was first beginning to write down flashes of insight about single objects. The poems which resulted from this practice occasioned Kenneth Burke's remark, in his review of *Sour Grapes*, that "what Williams sees he sees in a flash." Many of these "flashes," however, still found their way into Williams' larger, synthetic, poems, becoming part of a simultaneous field of objects instead of being allowed to stand on their own, and this was to be the case throughout Williams' career as a poet. Still, when Burke remarked about Williams' method that "there is the eye, and there is the thing upon which that eye alights; while the relationship between the two is a poem," and defined the poet's concern with "contact"

166

to mean "man with nothing but the thing and the feeling of that thing," he showed very clearly how close Williams had already to come to the ideal of the American "moment."[7] By concentrating on the significance of single objects, or the objective interrelationship between two units of material form, Williams shifted his attention from the image as subject to the object as image. Like Stieglitz he began to let the object speak for him by letting it speak for itself through his description of it and through the selection he made of its visual detail. Thus he learned that a poem about a single object need not necessarily be confined to two or three lines, but could, like "The Great Figure," for instance, expand according to the selection of relevant supporting detail the poet decided to include. That selection itself, however, should be representative of compressive extraction, for, as Williams now stressed, a characteristic of all good art "is its compactness. It is not, at its best, the mirror—which is too ready a symbol. It is life—but transmuted to another tighter form," and "restricted to essentials."[8]

Just as the prose sections of Williams' *Spring and All* (1923) reflect his study of the ideas of the writers of the Stieglitz group, so the poems in that book reflect his attempts to put these ideas to practice. Williams' famous little poem "The Red Wheelbarrow" (xxi of *Spring and All*)[9] is perhaps one of the best examples of the object-image poetry he was developing:

> so much depends
> upon

[7] Kenneth Burke, "Heaven's First Law," *The Dial*, LXXII (February 1922), 197-200.

[8] *Selected Essays*, 198.

[9] In the original edition of *Spring and All*, the poems did not have titles, but were given roman numerals. The titles were added with the publication of the *Collected Earlier Poems*.

a red wheel
barrow

glazed with rain
water

beside the white
chickens.

The poem is a perfect representation of the kind of painting or photography the Stieglitz group might have produced: it is a moment, caught at the point of its highest visual significance, in perfectly straightforward, "realistic," but highly selective detail; each word has its intrinsic evocative function, focusing the object and its essential structural relationship to its immediate surroundings in concrete terms. The words are facts, the direct linguistic equivalents to the visual object under scrutiny. The object, moreover, retains complete autonomy: it is in no way to be construed as a metaphor; rather, the very fact of its actual existence within the objective world, exactly according to the terms in which it is described, constitutes a statement about the objective world. Because the artist has focused upon the object under these particular circumstances, has *seen* the relationship it bears to his own position within the objective world, his statement of fact comes to represent his own feeling as well. As a result, "the baby glove of a Pharoah can be so presented as to bring tears to the eyes."[10] Thus poetry, like painting, can give the inmost concerns of man a tactile reality. By clearly focusing an element of reality, and stripping it of all inessential detail, we can finally succeed to "raise the place we inhabit to such an imaginative level that it shall have currency in the world

[10] *Selected Essays*, 122.

168

of the mind."[11] In the context of this visual emphasis, short comments by the poet are sometimes needed where a painting or a print, which in itself is already a visual object, needs only a frame, or nothing at all: Williams' comment "so much depends / upon" is the verbal equivalent to the very fact of the visual existence of a painting —which is itself a statement that much depends upon the object it portrays.

The poem "Spring and All" (i), one of the many poems about spring with which Williams liked to open his books, and one of the best, is a landscape, much like the brooding photographs in which Stieglitz presented elements of nature as equivalents to his innermost emotions:

> By the road to the contagious hospital
> under the surge of the blue
> mottled clouds driven from the
> northeast—a cold wind. Beyond, the
> waste of broad, muddy fields
> brown with dried weeds, standing and fallen
>
> patches of standing water
> the scattering of tall trees
>
> All along the road the reddish
> purplish, forked, upstanding, twiggy
> stuff of bushes and small trees
> with dead, brown leaves under them
> leafless vines—

Clarity of description, the poet's ability to present "outline of leaf," and a careful selection of natural detail, is the key to Williams' success here. The clouds, the dried

[11] "Memory Script of a Talk Delivered at Briarcliff Junior College, November 29, 1945," unpublished ms. in the Lockwood Memorial Library, State University of New York at Buffalo.

weeds, standing and fallen, the patches of standing
water, the tall trees—all are equivalents to feeling, expressive of the human condition. So are the reddish, purplish,
forked bushes along the road and the dead brown leaves,
the leafless vines, which constitute precisely the structural contrasts between vegetation and earth from which
Arthur Dove constructed so many of his best paintings.
Again, in terms of method, the description, especially in
the first part of the poem, is purely that of a visual, a
pictorial field, in which, as Williams says in one of the
last lines, "one by one objects are defined."

There is considerable similarity between this poem
and "The Farmer" (iii), a more conventional picture of
a farmer in his fields. Again the poem represents a single
image, the man placed against his soil:

> A cold wind ruffles the water
> among the browned weeds.
> On all sides
> the world rolls coldly away:
> black orchards
> darkened by the March clouds—

But as they were always to continue to do, literary
impulses were struggling against suppression in Williams.
He was too much grounded in the formal conventions
of writing to be able to delete the voice of the poet, his
subjective interpretation of the things seen. He found
it difficult to let the image speak for him without interference. He did not have at this time, and was never
entirely to have, the absolute confidence of the visual
artist, who knows that the image itself will be more
expressive than he could ever be. Consequently, in the
last lines of "The Farmer" the concrete materials of the
visual world are overtaken by Williams' conscious voice:

Down past the brushwood
bristling by
the rainsluiced wagonroad
looms the artist figure of
the farmer—composing
—antagonist

As Williams said almost despairingly at the end of
another poem from *Spring and All,* "The Black Winds"
(v):

How easy to slip
into the old mode, how hard to
cling firmly to the advance—

In many of the poems of this collection Williams indeed
tended to slip back into the old mode, even when he
set out to see and delineate a "Composition" (xii) consisting of a material object: "The red paper box / hinged
with cloth" lined "inside and out / with imitation /
leather" might suddenly become a vehicle for questions,
metaphors, and literary remarks about the nature of
eternity. Even when, as in "The Eyeglasses" (x) "the
universality of things" drew Williams

toward the candy
with melon flowers that open

about the edge of refuse
proclaiming without accent
the quality of the farmer's

shoulders and his daughter's
accidental skin, so sweet
with clover and the small

yellow cinquefoil in the
parched places . . .

171

even in such cases, the temptation might be too great to throw in a pleasant, euphonic line such as "tranquilly Titicaca," which had much more to do with his reading of Wallace Stevens' work than with his intended direct delineation of concrete materials. Literary elements like this very likely caused Stieglitz to maintain his reservations toward Williams' poetry.

Williams' personal realization of how hard it was to cling firmly to the advance and his consequent need to continue to study the example of the visual artists in developing the elements of his poetry, coupled with his admiration for certain paintings, photographs, and other works of art as objects of reality in their own right, caused him to continue the practice which he had initiated in such poems as "March": the close study of a particular work, or, indeed, the literal transmutation of a specific painting into a poem, just as Demuth was later to translate the verbal statement of "The Great Figure" into a painting. Methods such as this helped Williams in his efforts to adapt the visual qualities of painting to the verbal structure of his poetry. Poem ii of *Spring and All*, "A Pot of Flowers," for instance, is a literal rendering into poetry of Demuth's watercolor "Tuberoses," which was painted in 1922, and soon after became a part of Williams' own collection (Plate xx). The words Williams uses in his poem to describe the flowers are infused with the familiar brilliance of Demuth's colors: "mauve," "flame green" (a marvelous transliteration of the visual quality of young leaves), and "pink confused with white." Williams carefully describes how the petals, "radiant with transpiercing light" break out, as in Demuth's watercolor, above the leaves "reaching up their modest green / from the pot's rim." The fact that *Spring and All* was dedicated to Demuth indicates how deeply Williams knew himself to be indebted to the work of his friend. Later, in "The Crimson Cyclamen," the poet's stark, celebratory memorial to Demuth, the precise visual language he developed in studying the painter's work would allow him to write a poem in which the cycles of man's existence are expressed entirely in terms of Demuth's intensely real world of watercolor flowers.

"The Pot of Flowers" is not the only poem in *Spring and All* which is based on an actual painting. Poem vii, "The Rose," is a translation of Juan Gris's 1914 collage "Roses." During the years before America's entry into World War I, Gris had been virtually unknown to the New York avant garde, but after the war his work came to be featured prominently in such magazines as *The Little Review* and *The Dial*. His very personal brand of Cubism, which joined a clear love for the natural forms of concrete materials with the "orthodox" solidification of intangible spatial qualities, brought his work very close in conception to that of such American painters as Demuth and Sheeler. Like the Americans, and unlike Picasso and Braque, Gris continued to modulate the volumes of many of the objects he depicted according to the conventional, "realistic," painterly methods of presenting optical registration of three dimensional forms. By superimposing forms rendered in this fashion over planar constructions developed according to the Cubists' redistribution and intermodulation of visual elements, Gris obtained a synthesis of Realism and Cubism which is closely analogous to the synthesis of these two elements which Williams had achieved in some of his more successful poems. It is therefore not surprising that Williams felt a special affinity with this artist. Throughout the Twenties and beyond, Gris remained, with Demuth and Sheeler, among Williams' favorite painters.

In many of Gris's works there is a very photographic

173

quality of light. This, together with his precise delineation of objects and volumes, allowed him to maintain the integrity of his forms in a way Stieglitz would, and undoubtedly did, approve wholeheartedly. The collage "Roses" is a case in point: the roses are photographic, cut out of a flower catalogue perhaps, or from a poster, and literally pasted into the composition. Williams, by his own admission, saw only a black and white reproduction of this collage, and in black and white the fact that this work is a collage is obscured. As a result the brilliantly hard-edged shapes attain an even more striking sharpness (Plate xxi). It thus became an especially useful exercise for Williams to turn this visual object into a poem of precise observation, consisting of words with a quality as real and hard as the reproduction from which Williams took his poem:

> The rose is obsolete
> but each petal ends in
> an edge, the double facet
> cementing the grooved
> columns of air—The edge
> cuts without cutting
> meets—nothing—renews
> itself in metal or porcelain—

Williams translates the tactile reality of the rose into words which by the very intensity of their tactile associations force us to consider the rose completely in terms of the concrete existence it represents, rather than allowing us to give it a metaphorical, or otherwise literary "significance":

> Somewhere the sense
> makes copper roses
> steel roses—

174

And:

> From the petal's edge a line starts
> that being of steel
> infinitely fine, infinitely
> rigid penetrates
> the Milky Way
> without contact—lifting
> from it—neither hanging
> nor pushing—
>
> The fragility of the flower
> unbruised
> penetrates space.

The fact that Williams in this poem succeeded to a large extent in avoiding a discursive personal interpretation of the "meaning" of Gris's collage adds to the success of his translation. Gris's work, as a completely objective conjunction of material forms, presents, in the very nature of this conjunction, the aesthetic-emotional construct through which the artist's personal perception is transmitted to the viewer. This leaves the viewer free to interpret that perception according to his own patterns of visual understanding, without having to adjust himself through an enforced meaning to the artist's obstructive intellectualization of his initial and all-important subconscious understanding. Similarly, Williams, in his selection and description of visual elements, intimates the nature of his personal understanding of Gris's collage, wishes us to see that work through the particular selection of his eyes, but allows us to develop our own understanding of the visual construct which constitutes his poem, because he describes and delineates, rather than imposing a specific, unambiguous, verbal interpretation of meaning. Williams breaks away from description to

175

direct interpretation: first when he begins by saying that "the rose is obsolete," and second when he asserts that

> The rose carried weight of love
> but love is at an end—of roses
> It is at the edge of the
> petal that love waits

But both these instances of Williams' interpretive interference are minor, and not sufficiently specific to restrict the focus of the reader's personal intuitive apprehension. Williams, in other words, has left the poem, "sharper, neater, more cutting / figured in majolica," to "the broken plate / glazed with a rose."

In terms of the method of his poems, the nature of their focus, and the development of his subject-matter, Williams showed in *Spring and All* the progressive redirection of his poetry according to the structural patterns advocated by the painters he admired most. But the theoretical influence of the writers of the Stieglitz group, which had such a central importance to the prose sections of that book, also finds its echo in the poems. "To Elsie" (xviii), Williams' poem about America, reflects the concepts about the nature of life in this country which Hartley, Frank, and Rosenfeld had expounded in their essays, and which Williams was to reiterate in *In the American Grain*: The reason why "the pure products of America," such as Elsie Borden, "go crazy," is because they are rootless. They have "imaginations which have no / peasant traditions to give them / character." Consequently they have no emotion

> save numbed terror
>
> under some hedge of choke-cherry
> or viburnum—
> which they cannot express—

Williams here left the reference of "which" deliberately ambiguous, so that it becomes clear that not only the numbed terror is inexpressible to them but also the hedge of choke-cherry and the viburnum. They are incapable of seeing, of understanding nature, the organic object. Girls like Elsie, who have a slight, instinctive longing for contact, for an understanding of the objective world, because they were born "perhaps / with a dash of Indian blood," will go insane due to their inability to establish this contact, due to the desolation, disease, and murder with which they are hemmed round. But such an Elsie can, "with broken brain," express the truth about us, showing us how we behave

> as if the earth under our feet
> were
> an excrement of some sky
>
> and we degraded prisoners
> destined
> to hunger until we eat filth
>
> while the imagination strains
> after deer
> going by fields of goldenrod in
>
> the stifling heat of September

These are the things which destroy the American. Until he can force his imagination to take account of, rejoice in, the pure, immediate reality of the earth under his feet, and so establish his contact with his own, local, consciousness, instead of letting himself strain after the otherwhere of "deer / going by fields of goldenrod," until such a time, the American is doomed to go crazy. In the meantime,

> It is only in isolate flecks that

something
is given off

No one
to witness
and adjust, no one to drive the car

The poem is primarily a diagnosis; its solution is implied. But there are the isolate flecks of understanding which intimate some hope for the future, if only someone can be found to "drive the car." Doubtless Williams considered his poetry a record of the "isolate flecks" and one of the means by which America could be driven to understanding, just as the photographs of Stieglitz and the work of his painters fulfilled that function in their own media.

Clearly Williams by this time had been infected with the photographer's sense of mission and firm belief in the possibility of a new and independently "local" America. It is in this spirit that throughout the Twenties he continued to improve and refine the "American" qualities in his poetry, which meant, in effect, that he continued to develop the various possibilities of presenting the material object, closely perceived, and recorded through a selection of its most salient features. Sometimes, as we have seen, he constructed poems which consisted of only a single object within its environment. But the possibilities for this kind of poetry are much more limited than they are in painting. If the poet elaborates on the qualities of the object in question beyond the essentials which contain the significant vision—if the poet begins to fill in too many secondary patterns—he defeats his original purpose, which should always be to present the object in terms of its most telling elements, and as a result the poem loses the "moment," loses its quintessential immediacy. It is therefore only occasionally that Williams created such poems. They do, however, occur with some consistency throughout his work. But usually the object would take its place as a more or less independent unit within the larger field of a composite poem, because ultimately for Williams the primary importance of the object in poetry was in the fact that it was perceived and presented as it actually existed, and would thus enhance the reality of the poem as "thing itself." Thus the poem would become an integral element in the complex structure of contact between man and the material world:

> That is why boxing matches and
> Chinese poems are the same—That is why
> Hartley praises Miss Wirt . . .[12]

The Descent of Winter, a group of poems interspersed with prose statements, and in form much like *Spring and All*, is representative of the conscientious fashion in which Williams pursued his quest for a completely objective mode of writing. The collection was published in Pound's magazine *The Exile* in 1928, and showed how Williams' emphasis on observation had populated his imagination with such a plethora of materials from observed reality that even when he ostensibly attempted to "reason," to speak from the intellect, his mind would swerve away from abstract conceptions, back to the reassurance of tangible things:

"10/23 I will make a big, serious portrait of my time. The brown and creamwhite block of Mexican onyx has

---

[12] "The Black Winds" (v), *Spring and All*. In *Adventures in the Arts* Marsden Hartley devotes a celebratory chapter to the circus equestrienne May Wirth, a young woman whose agility and beauty came in Hartley's eyes to stand for "the beautiful plastic of the body, harmonically arranged for personal delight," and thus for the most perfect expression of the integration of man as natural object with material reality.

a poorly executed replica of the Aztec calendar on one of its dicefacets the central circle being a broadnosed face with projected hanging tongue the sun perhaps though why the tongue is out I do not know unless to taste or gasp in the heat, its own heat, to say it's hot and is the sun. Puebla, Mexico, Calendario Azteca, four words are roughly engraved in the four corners where the circle leaves spaces on the square diceface this is America some years after the original, the art of writing is to do work so excellent that by its excellence it repels all idiots but idiots are like leaves and excellence of any sort is a tree when the leaves fall the tree is naked and the wind thrashes it till it howls it cannot get a book published it can only get poems into certain magazines that are suppressed because because waving waving waving waving waving waving tick tack tic tock tadick there is not excellence without the vibrant rhythm of a poem and poems are small and tied and gasping they eat gasoline, they all ate gasoline and died, they died of—there is a hole in the wood and all I say brings to mind the rock shingles of Cherbourg, on the new houses they have put cheap tile which overlaps but the old roofs had flat stones sides steep but of stones fitted together and that is love there is no portrait without that has not turned to prose love is my hero who does no live, a man, but speaks of it every day. . . ."[13]

Much of *The Descent of Winter* is consequently made up of pure description, often, as in the passage quoted, the result of a multiform reality closely observed, and presented in the broken pattern of quick notation Williams first developed under the influence of Simultaneism

[13] Williams, "The Descent of Winter," 35-36. (The prose sections of "The Descent of Winter" have been reprinted in the *Selected Essays* as "Notes in Diary Form," 62-74, and erroneously presented as "not previously published.")

in *Kora in Hell*. All he was concerned with at this point was to find "the truth of the object." He emphasized that "the good poetry is where the vividness comes up 'true' . . . ; poetry should strive for nothing else, this vividness alone, *per se*, for itself. The realization of this has its own internal fire that is 'like' nothing. Therefore the bastardy of the simile. That thing, the vividness which is poetry by itself, makes the poem. This is modern, not the saga. There are no sagas—only trees now, animals, engines: There's that."[14]

The poems in *The Descent of Winter*, perhaps even more than those in *Spring and All*, show how close Williams' conception had come to the central concerns of the Stieglitz group toward the end of the Twenties. They are all celebrations of the *ding an sich*. "I know a good print when I see it," Williams asserts in one of the prose sections, referring to the photography of Sheeler. Alluding to one of Stieglitz's practices he adds: "It is the neck of a man, the nose of a woman." Williams' focus in *The Descent of Winter* is just that: "on the polished straws of the dead grass a scroll of crimson paper—not yet rained on," or "on hot days / the sewing machine / whirling," "a beard . . . not of stone but particular hairs purpleblack," or

> a white birch
> with yellow leaves
> and few
> and loosely hung

In their precision and concise mode of presentation these poems recall one which Williams published in *Manuscripts* in 1922:

> My luv
> is like

[14] *Ibid.*, 46-47.

a
greenglass insulator
on
a blue sky[15]

This poem associates itself vividly with the sharply delineated early studies of machinery by Demuth and Sheeler. Indeed, the steel-like purity of shape and absolute, razor-sharp quality of line in the work of these painters, and in such works as Juan Gris's collage "Roses," together with the equally sharp clarity of the colors they used, doubtless formed the visual stimulus for Williams' move towards precision of expression. The work of these artists taught Williams to see the objective world with photographic precision and to translate its materials into words of equal clarity. Later, writing about Sheeler, he emphasized that this artist was "particularly valuable because of the bewildering directness of his vision, without blur," and because he showed that "the world of the artist is not gossamer but steel and plaster."[16] Evans, the protagonist of A Voyage to Pagany (1928) and a thinly disguised portrait of Williams himself, sees the world entirely in terms of such photographic qualities: "The world existed in his eyes, recognized itself ecstatically there . . . , everywhere he saw reality, split, creviced, multiplied. The brilliant hardness of the world, clear, full of color and outline, depth, shadow, reaffirming light, filled him with security and contentment."[17]

In studying the work of these men, therefore, Williams learned how to combine the elements of visual composition which he had taken from his study of

[15] William Carlos Williams, "Two Poems," Manuscripts, 1 (February 1922), 15. These two poems have never been reprinted.
[16] Selected Essays, 231-32.
[17] A Voyage to Pagany, 119.

French painting with the subject matter and visual accuracy of his American contemporaries. Like his friend Demuth he learned to combine the study of the qualities of place and the objects representing the universality of place (the "local" being the only "universal") with the structural innovations of "the forces from the outside," as he was to say in his tribute to Stieglitz. In his best poems the result is a mixture of concrete, steel-edged, "visible" words and an equally sharp definition of light and shadow, such as in "Between Walls," a poem of the late Twenties:

BETWEEN WALLS

the back wings
of the

hospital where
nothing

will grow lie
cinders

in which shine
the broken

pieces of a green
bottle

This poem has much of the visual simplicity and purity of line to be found in such paintings as Sheeler's "Bucks County Barns," discussed earlier. It contains, as Williams said about Sheeler's work, "the abstract if you will, but left by the artist integral with its native detail."[18]

In the various styles of the painters of the Stieglitz group, as well as in the work of the photographer himself, Williams found a wide range of visual constructs which could be adapted in his poetry. Many of his more

[18] *Selected Essays*, 233.

broken, fragmented poems, which at first may seem to be influenced by impulses stemming from the Dadaists, will show themselves, on closer examination, to have less to do with Dada as such than with the adaptation of Cubist and Dadaist methods to the expression of very positive, celebratory presentations of the organic universe by such painters as John Marin and Arthur Dove. Marin was an early favorite of Williams, and it is possible that "Spring Strains" was to some extent influenced by Marin's work as well as by European Cubism. The language of Marin's statement about his New York watercolors, his sense of "pull forces," his vision of great powers at work, "pushing, pulling, sideways, downward, upwards," would seem to find an echo in the language of "Spring Strains." Some of the fragmented compositions of *Spring and All* show the influence of the "skyscraper soup," which Williams associates in "Young Love" (ix) with Marin's work. Later many of the poems present elements of landscape in a fashion very similar to the visual qualities of Marin's quick, dancing watercolors, which in a few brush strokes accurately evoke a plant, the horizon, sun, or waves, real things brought together in a timeless rhythm of color and line. In "Flowers by the Sea," a poem of the late Twenties, it is hard to forego the impression that Williams' observations are taken from one of that painter's watercolors rather than from a landscape personally seen:

> When over the flowery, sharp pasture's
> edge, unseen, the salt ocean
>
> lifts its form—chicory and daisies
> tied, released, seem hardly flowers alone
>
> but color and the movement—or the shape
> perhaps—of restlessness, whereas

184

the sea is circled and sways
peacefully upon its plantlike stem

The instances in which poems by Williams resemble
works by these painters are too frequent to list. From
them he learned how to fix a scene or an object and
describe it in terms of its most essential, most visually
significant, elements. Obviously he might therefore, in
describing an object or scene he actually saw, very well
write a poem which closely resembled one or another of
their works, without having such a painting directly in
mind. Often similarity is due primarily to stylistic and
thematic affinity. Williams, however, was convinced that
only by adhering closely to the concrete visual world of
the painters could he avoid the deadening conventionality and colorless monotony of most poetry. He therefore tried to escape what he considered to be the inherent
artificiality of language by infusing it with concrete
things. His poem "This Florida: 1924," is a very clear
statement of this:

> . . . I am sick of rime—
> The whole damned town
>
> is riming up one street
> and down another, yet there is
> the rime of her white teeth
>
> the rime of glasses
> at my plate, the ripple time
> the rime her fingers make—
>
> And we thought to escape rime
> by imitation of the senseless
> unarrangement of wild things—
>
> the stupidest rime of all—
> Rather, Hibiscus,

185

let me examine

those varying shades
of orange, clear as an electric
bulb on fire

or powdery with sediment—
matt, the shades and textures
of a Cubist picture

the charm
of fish by Hartley, orange
of ale and lilies

orange of topaz, orange of red hair
orange of curaçoa
orange of the Tiber

turbid, orange of the bottom
rocks in Maine rivers
orange of mushrooms

By 1924, then, if we accept Williams' dating of this poem, the poet had renounced not only the literary conventions, such as rime, but also the equally artificial "imitation of the senseless / unarrangement of wild things" which was then current in certain avant garde literary circles. Instead he wanted to concentrate in his poetry on examining and emulating either "the shades and textures of a Cubist picture," or "the charm / of fish by Hartley."

Williams, in other words, now fully equated his role as a poet with the function of the visual artist. His concept of the shaping force of the imagination both stemmed from and subsequently reinforced that attitude. The imagination made snapshots of the material world, as it were, thus fixing the objects of existence on the film of the artist's memory, until he could analyze their ele-

186

ments and select their most significant details, to create
through his art an equivalent to the emotion which
moved him at the moment of vision, thus allowing that
moment to be suspended in an eternal present of universal significance. Many years later, during the last years
of his life, Williams was to reaffirm this belief in the
poem "Bird," from *Pictures From Brueghel* (1962):

> Bird with outstretched
> wings poised
> inviolate unreaching
>
> yet reaching
> your image this November
> planes
>
> to a stop
> miraculously fixed in my
> arresting eyes.

The elimination of the non-essential, the clear focus
on the thing itself, necessary because there were no ideas
except in things, meant for Williams as much as for the
Stieglitz group the elimination of all reference to human
figures if the scene in focus involved only non-human
objects, unless these figures were a necessary part of the
scene fixed by the imagination, or unless human forms
or qualities were part of its essential concrete visual significance. Of course many of Williams' poems deal
directly with people or their actions, but in many others
only the eye was necessary to analyze and arrange nature
into its most accurate visual parts, as in this Hartley-like
still-life from the Twenties, "Sea-trout and Butterfish":

> The contours and the shine
> hold the eye—caught and lying
>
> orange-finned and the two
> half its size, pout-mouthed

> beside it on the white dish—
> Silver scales, the weight
>
> quick tails
> whipping the streams aslant
>
> The eye comes down eagerly
> unravelled of the sea
>
> separates this from that
> and the fine fins' sharp spines

In studying the work of the painters, Williams also became aware of the structural implications of the movement of objects within the visual space of a painting. Writing poems in direct study of such works as Demuth's "Tuberoses," he had to find a satisfactory equivalent in his poetry to the manner in which the eye, in exploring a painting as visual object, registers its elements in a specific pattern, which is determined by the emphasis which the painter has given to the various parts of his picture. This pattern endows the painting with a quality of autonomous, organic, movement. In his attempt to adapt this element of the visual experience to his poetry Williams tried to present the details of the object under his scrutiny according to a very deliberate sequence which would approximate the pattern the eye traces on the visual field of a carefully composed painting. Many years after he had first begun to be concerned with this aspect of composition Williams wrote a poem, "Raindrops on a Briar," in which he described what he had learned:

> I, a writer, at one time hipped on
> painting, did not consider
> the effects, painting,
> for that reason, static, on
>
> the contrary, the stillness of

the objects—the flowers, the gloves—
freed them precisely by that
from a necessity merely to move

in space as if they had been—
not children! but the thinking male
or the charged and deliver-
ing female frantic with ecstasies;

served rather to present, for me,
a more pregnant motion: a
series of varying leaves
clinging still, let us say, to

the cat-briar after last night's
storm, its waterdrops
ranged upon the arching stems
irregularly as an accompaniment.

Many of Williams' poems of the Twenties show that
this awareness had been an essential feature in their
organization. The swift, linear exploration of organic
form through an enumeration of facets which was determined in its order by the structural qualities of the form
under scrutiny became a basic organizing factor in his
work. Such a structure allowed him to avoid the lack of
a precise focus which had marred his earliest attempts
at still-life such as the poem "Daisy," discussed earlier.
The poem "Young Sycamore," first published in *The
Dial* in 1927, is a good example of the unity Williams'
poems could attain if they followed this principle of
linear movement:

I must tell you
this young tree
whose round and firm trunk
between the wet

189

pavement and the gutter
(where water
is trickling) rises
bodily

into the air with
one undulant
thrust half its height—
and then

dividing and waning
sending out
young branches on
all sides—

hung with cocoons
it thins
till nothing is left of it
but two

eccentric knotted
twigs
bending forward
hornlike at the top

The poem has a very precise linear movement which finds its logical conclusion in the description of the tree's top branches. At the same time it remains fixed within the compass of a single object, leaving the object to express its own universal regenerative significance. What makes this poem especially interesting is that it would seem to be a minute description of the tree in Stieglitz's photograph "Spring Showers" (Plate IX): Williams' description of the tree in its environment of pavement, gutter, and trickling water, as well as his emphasis on its young branches hung with cocoons, and on the trunk which suddenly divides itself at half its height, makes it correspond so minutely to the facts of Stieglitz's photograph that the possibility of coincidence seems highly unlikely.

Williams, in fact, seems to have come to the conclusion that he need not limit his poetry to a description of the incidents fixed by the camera eye of his own imagination, but that he might just as effectively make poems out of the visual records of experience presented in those paintings, drawings, or photographs which caught his fancy. Beginning with the Twenties an ever larger part of his writing began to consist of such materials. His stories and essays are filled with descriptions, often fragmentary, of pictures remembered, and in many of his poems we come across sudden thumbnail sketches of specific works by his favorite painters. Not infrequently, as in "Young Sycamore," he would make a painting the basis for a whole poem. Sometimes he would openly acknowledge such a poem's derivation, or he would give an oblique hint, such as in the title of his poem "Classic Scene," which is based on Sheeler's painting "Classic Landscape" (Plate xviii); but usually he would give no indication at all that a poem was based on a painting or photograph, rather than on an incident taken directly from reality.

Williams was "a great gallery goer" during the Twenties and Thirties. He "saw Stieglitz often and if there was an exhibit of the French masters or any show at the Modern Museum or the Whitney gallery," he was sure to be there.[19] It is therefore very likely that among the many poems which seem based on personal observation of elements in nature or the city, a number are in fact records of what the poet observed in the visual constructions of other artists. For Williams, who, after all, regarded a work of art as a perfectly autonomous, perfectly "real" object, this must have seemed a legitimate

[19] *Autobiography*, 240.

191

practice, since all things in the objective world were potential subjects for his poetry. Moreover, he undoubtedly reasoned, a poem which takes its inspiration from a specific painting depends as much on the poet's personal selection of detail as a poem based on nature. The poet's description may, in fact, focus on a single feature of the painting which might go unnoticed by other viewers, and hence continue the pattern of enlightenment initiated by the painter. No wonder then that some of Williams' poems recall paintings by Marsden Hartley, others Marin watercolors, still others photographs from a magazine or book. Ultimately the factual origin of the material for these poems matters little. Important, however, is that they show how literally Williams came to equate the writing of poetry with the processes of painting, how completely he came to see the objective world as an unending sequence of framed images which had only to be isolated from the stream of things, either by himself or by one of the painters he admired, to become potential material for a poem.

Williams, then, during the first twenty years of his long career as a poet, was not, as he has been portrayed, an isolated figure singlehandedly charging into new, unheard-of areas of aesthetic experience. He was, moreover, by no means the only one fighting for neglected American values in an utterly indifferent world, as he sometimes liked to portray himself. He was rather one of a clearly defined group of American artists who were brought together by their natural inclinations and the accident of age, under the leadership of an older contemporary with clearly defined values. He was part of a generation which, unjustly, has been grouped with those writers whose debut falls in the early Twenties, and who took no part in the explorations of 1913-1917. As Lewis Mumford has remarked, people like Paul Rosenfeld,

Randolph Bourne, Marianne Moore, and Williams, let alone Stieglitz, were part of the generation preceding Edmund Wilson, E. E. Cummings, Hemingway, and F. Scott Fitzgerald. They did not belong to the rather self-consciously "lost" generation of the Twenties. "The older group," Mumford writes, "fiercely rejected the cherished idols of middle-class America, the very America that had sought to direct their footsteps from the stormswept beach of contemporary life to the elevated boardwalk of respectability. They challenged the sordid, mechanistic, venal hypocritical life that underlay the tepid spiritual manifestations of the genteel tradition. Despite their rejections they were, in the main, deeply affirmative personalities, full of generous hopes for the new American promise."[20] These men did not run to Europe to escape America; they set out instead to express themselves through America, for the very reasons outlined in this study. T.S. Eliot and Ezra Pound were therefore far more appropriate heroes for the Twenties than William Carlos Williams, who scoffed at the expatriates. The attitude of most of the younger group toward the older men can be summarized in W. C. Blum's disparaging comment about Williams' *Contact*, in his "American Letter" in a 1921 issue of *The Dial*: "To use a theory of this sort as a test for art is stupid. Who is there, I don't care how illiterate, who can say whether a given piece of writing shows contact with the writer's environment?"[21]

Failure to recognize the importance of the pervasive influence of both European painting and American artists on the development of Williams' poetry during

[20] Lewis Mumford, "Lyric Wisdom," in *Paul Rosenfeld: Voyager In The Arts.*

[21] W. C. Blum, "American Letter," *The Dial*, LXX (May 1921), 562-68.

the first two decades of his career as a poet has caused students of his work to put an undue emphasis on later and parallel, or secondary, influences. Too often, moreover, a lack of respect for chronology, encouraged by Williams himself, who deliberately confused the order of his *Collected Earlier Poems,* has obscured the very specific pattern in which the poet's early work evolved. Some critics, in fact, have seen Williams' interest in painting as influencing only the poetry of his later years, while others have portrayed him inaccurately as an isolated figure, "in secret alliance with little known painters," artists who, "unknown to him, were shaping in the rickety garrets of Montmartre the artifacts of a new era." Such romantic fictions tend to ignore the specific pattern of influences which links Williams' work with painting. Certainly painting was by no means the only determinant in the development of his poetry, but it is by far the most important source for the structure and themes of his work. Ezra Pound, Whitman, and Gertrude Stein, to name just a few, undoubtedly contributed to Williams' development, but their part must be considered secondary to the role played by painting in general, and figures such as Alfred Stieglitz in particular.

Williams' dominant characteristics were his so curiously literal mind, which made him capable of seeing poetry almost entirely in terms of painting, and his tendency to adapt the ideas and creations of others to his own use. He did not have much theoretical acumen and it was his good fortune to find others whose inclinations were similar to his own when he needed guidance. Ultimately his great merit, and his role as an original and influential poet, depend on his extraordinary single-minded tenacity in attempting to turn poetry into a form of painting. For by trying to do so he pointed out a possible method for the use which can be made in poetry

194

of fragmentation, immediacy, condensation of imagery, and simple, precise diction. Other poets among his contemporaries—Marianne Moore and Wallace Stevens, for instance—expressed an initial desire to become painters, and painting obviously had an important influence on their work too. But Williams succeeded far better than they did in escaping the literary qualities, the tendencies to interpret and philosophize, which removes their work from painting.

The qualities of immediacy and visual precision which Williams learned from the painters, and which he developed so tenaciously during the 1910's and 1920's, remained important features of his work throughout the rest of his life. As Williams grew older, other painters and other movements in both arts and literature than the ones discussed here became influential to the further development of his work. But the initial impact of Cubism and the ideas and visual structures of the Stieglitz group remained even then the most important shaping factors. Any study of the later poems should therefore take very careful account of the role which they played in determining the form as well as the content of the later works. To discuss the nature of the influences from the visual arts on *The Wedge, Paterson, A Journey to Love,* or *Pictures from Brueghel* would be beyond the scope of this study, and would, moreover, tend to redundancy. But in these, as in all of Williams' other writings, the development of his method, the nature of his focus, and the theoretical basis for his poetic concerns with structure as discussed in these pages, will be seen to serve a central function. Such continued preoccupations of his later years as objectivism, the expression of local consciousness, the search for a new measure, and his subsequent discovery of the variable foot are a direct result of his initial fascination with the visual arts, and his subsequent attempts to cope with their structural implications. Moreover, as *Pictures from Brueghel*, many short poems, such as "Tribute to the Painters," and, most of all, *Paterson* V testify, Williams was not merely "at one time hipped on painting," but remained so all his life.

In a thorough study of Williams, therefore, the poet's initial fascination with Cubism, and his subsequent long-lasting association with the Stieglitz group, should not be ignored. It should be remembered that when Arthur Dove, in 1925, listed the basic principles underlying the work of the artists around Stieglitz, he was speaking for Williams as well:

A WAY TO LOOK AT THINGS
We have not yet made shoes that fit like water
Nor clothes that fit like water
Nor thoughts that fit like air.
There is much to be done—
Works of nature are abstract.
They do not lean on other things for meanings.
The sea-gull is not like the sea
Nor the sun like the moon.
The sun draws water from the sea.
The clouds are not like either one—
They do not keep one form forever.
That the mountain looks like a face is accidental.[22]

In this attitude, with its rejection of metaphor and fancy "literary" posturing in art, and its strong affirmation of belief in the independent validity of natural things, of the thing itself, Williams found the anchoring element for his own pursuits. The explorations of the seven artists in the exhibition for which Dove's poem served as official manifesto represented, in the words of a contempo-

[22] Quoted in *America and Alfred Stieglitz*, 121.

rary critic, "nothing less than the discovery of America's independent role in the history of art,"[23] and as such they provided Williams with the theoretical and visual means with which to articulate the unformed emotional values which made him realize his fellowship with these men. Because his realm was words, not paint, he translated the elements of visual experience which animated the work of these artists into their verbal counterparts. But he remained always a painter at heart, convinced that he might have been much more articulate had he been able to "dispense with those damn words altogether." He persisted until the very end of his life in his belief in the communicative power of the visual arts, and in his distrust of language when it was not the reflection of a thing, but a literary, an intellectual abstraction. In what may be one of the last poems he ever wrote, published in the year of his death in the *Hudson Review*, he made a final effort to explain once more the reason for this attitude:

> STILL LIFES
> All poems can be represented by
> still lifes not to say
> water-colors, the violence of
> the Iliad lends itself to an arrangement
> of narcissi in a jar.
> The slaughter of Hector by Achilles
> can well be shown by them
> casually assembled yellow upon white
> radiantly making a circle
> swart strokes violently given
> in more or less haphazard disarray

The visual power of a work by a good painter, in even such a relatively slight medium as watercolor, is such that

[23] Arnold Rönnebeck, quoted *ibid.*

the elemental human emotions may be expressed in it with an accuracy equivalent to the achievement of the greatest poem of western civilization. Such matters of crucial societal importance as the slaughter of Hector by Achilles—which, to make actual and significant in words, Homer has to describe so laboriously—can easily be expressed in the visual arts merely by means of the artist's intuitive understanding of the equivalent significance of certain visual lines found in narcissi, and his ability to capture these lines in a few "swart strokes violently given / in more or less haphazard disarray." This poem, in other words, is a final statement, on Williams' part, about what he considered to be the limitations of language in comparison to the possibilities inherent in the visual arts. By imitating the methods and theories of painting, he tried to diminish the gap between the two media. He believed that if he could only succeed in approximating the concentration of statement which could be found in even a simple watercolor, he might be able to turn words into visual objects, into those hieroglyphics of a new speech which he considered far more powerful, far more intense, than any existing language. What he tried to do was perhaps impossible, but he nearly succeeded, and the intensity of his struggle makes the visual power of his best poems all the more real.

SELECTIVE BIBLIOGRAPHY

I. WILLIAM CARLOS WILLIAMS

N.B.: The Lockwood Memorial Library of the State University of New York at Buffalo and the Yale University Library have important Williams mss. collections which contain considerable material illuminating the nature of Williams' interest in the visual arts.

A. BOOKS AND ARTICLES BY WILLIAM CARLOS WILLIAMS

Poems (Rutherford 1909).

The Tempers (London 1913).

"Invocations," *The Egoist*, I, 16 (August 15, 1914). A group of early poems.

Al Que Quiere! A Book of Poems (Boston, 1917).

"America, Whitman, and the Art of Poetry," *The Poetry Journal*, VIII, 1 (November 1917), 27-36.

"Notes from a Talk on Poetry," *Poetry*, XIV (July 1919), 211-16.

"Four Foreigners," *The Little Review*, VI, 5 (September 1919), 36-39.

Kora in Hell: Improvisations (Boston 1920).

Sour Grapes (Boston 1921).

"Two Poems," *Manuscripts*, 1 (February 1922), 15.

"The Reader Critic," *The Little Review*, IX, 3 (1922), 59-60. A letter to the editor.

Spring and All (Dijon, France, 1923).

The Great American Novel (1923), reprinted in *American Short Novels*, ed. R. P. Blackmur (New York 1960), 307-43.

In the American Grain (1925), paperback reprint, with an introduction by Horace Gregory (New York 1956).

A Voyage to Pagany (New York 1928).

"The Descent of Winter," *The Exile*, 4 (Autumn 1928), 30-69.

"Impasse and Imagery," *The Dial*, LXXXV (November 1928), 431-32.

A Novelette and Other Prose (1921-1931) (Toulon, France 1932).

The Collected Later Poems (New York 1950).

The Collected Earlier Poems (New York 1951).

Autobiography (New York 1951).

Selected Essays (New York 1954).

"Tribute to John Marin," *M: The Catalogue of the John Marin Memorial Exhibition at UCLA* (Los Angeles 1955).

The Selected Letters of William Carlos Williams, ed. John C. Thirlwall (New York 1957).

"The Lost Poems of William Carlos Williams or The Past Recaptured," *New Directions 16* (1957), 3-45. Collected and edited by John C. Thirlwall.

I Wanted To Write a Poem, ed. Edith Heal (Boston 1958).

The Farmers' Daughters, the Collected Short Stories (New York 1961).

Pictures from Brueghel and Other Poems (New York 1962).

Paterson I-V (New York 1963).

"The Art of Poetry: An Interview with William Carlos Williams," by Stanley Koehler, *The Paris Review,* 32 (Summer-Fall 1964), 111-51.

B. Magazines Edited by William Carlos Williams

Contact (New York, December 1920-June 1923); 5 issues.

Contact (New Series), (1932); 3 issues.

C. Critical Studies of William Carlos Williams

Useful bibliographies of secondary sources can be found in John Malcolm Brinnin, *William Carlos Williams* (Minneapolis 1963); Linda Welshimer Wagner, *The Poems of William Carlos Williams* (Middletown 1964); and *William Carlos Williams: A Collection of Critical Essays,* ed. J. Hillis Miller (Englewood Cliffs 1966). The special section, "A Gathering for William Carlos Williams," in *The Massachusetts Review,* III, 2 (Winter 1962) contains a reproduction of a self-portrait in oil by Williams.

· II. ALFRED STIEGLITZ, THE STIEGLITZ GROUP AND 291

N.B.: The Stieglitz Archive at the Yale University Library contains much correspondence between Stieglitz and a large number of artists and writers, as well as many catalogues, magazines, and newspaper clippings dealing with Stieglitz or members of the Stieglitz circle. A "key" set of Stieglitz's photographs is in the National Gallery in Washington.

Sherwood Anderson, "Alfred Stieglitz," *The New Republic*, xxxii (October 25, 1922), 215-17.

Egmont Arens, "Alfred Stieglitz: His Cloud Pictures," *Playboy*, 9 (July 1924), 15.

Art Galleries, University of California, *Catalogue of the John Marin Memorial Exhibition*, with contributions by Duncan Phillips, William Carlos Williams, Dorothy Norman, MacKinley Helm, and Frederick S. Wight (Los Angeles 1955).

E. M. Benson, "Alfred Stieglitz: The Man and the Book." *The American Magazine of Art*, xxviii (January 1935), 36-42.

Guido Bruno, "The Passing of 291," *Pearson's Magazine*, xxxviii, 9 (March 1918), 402-03.

Doris Bry, *An Exhibition of Photographs by Alfred Stieglitz* (Washington 1958). National Gallery of Art Exhibition Catalogue.

———, *Alfred Stieglitz: Photographer* (Boston 1965). Contains a large selection of Stieglitz's photographs.

W. B. Bryan, "Stieglitz," *Twice a Year*, v-vi (1942), 132-33.

Charles H. Caffin, "Photography as a Fine Art: The Work of Alfred Stieglitz," *Everybody's Magazine*, iv, 20 (April 1901).

———, *Photography as a Fine Art* (New York 1901).

James B. Carrington, "Night Photography," *Scribner's* (November 1897).

Huntley Carter, "Two-Ninety-One," *The Egoist*, iii, 3 (March 1916).

R. M. Coates, "Alfred Stieglitz," *The New Yorker*, XXIII (June 21, 1947), 43-45.

Thomas Craven, "Stieglitz, Old Master of the Camera," *Saturday Evening Post*, CCXVI (January 8, 1944), 14-15.

Robert Doty, *Photo-Secession: Photography as a Fine Art* (Rochester 1960).

Georgia Engelhard, "Alfred Stieglitz, Master Photographer," *American Photography*, XXXIX (April 1945), 8-12.

―――, "Grand Old Man," *American Photography*, XLIV (May 1950), 18-19 ff.

Guy Eglington, "Art and Other Things," *International Studio*, LXXIX (May 1924), 148-51.

R. Flint, "What is 291? Alfred Stieglitz and Modern Art in the United States," *Christian Science Monitor Weekly Magazine Section* (November 17, 1937), 5.

Waldo, Frank, *Our America* (New York 1919).

―――, *The Rediscovery of America* (New York 1929).

Clarence I. Freed, "Alfred Stieglitz: Genius of the Camera," *The American Hebrew* (January 18, 1924).

Marsden Hartley, *Adventures in the Arts* (New York 1921).

MacKinley Helm, "John Marin," *Atlantic Monthly*, CLXXIX (February 1947), 76-81.

―――, *John Marin* (Boston 1948).

Dorothy Rylander Johnson, *Arthur Dove: The Years of Collage* (College Park, Maryland 1967). University of Maryland Art Gallery Exhibition Catalogue.

O. Larkin, "Alfred Stieglitz and '291,'" *The Magazine of Art*, XL (May 1947), 178-83.

J. Nilsen Laurvik, "Alfred Stieglitz, Pictorial Photographer," *International Studio*, XLIV, 174 (August 1911), 21-27.

F. J. Mather, "Photographer and Champion of Art," *Saturday Review*, XI (December 8, 1934), 337.

Henry McBride, "Modern Art," *The Dial*, LXX (April 1921), 480-82.

Elizabeth McCausland, *Marsden Hartley* (Amsterdam 1961). Amsterdam Stedelijk Museum Exhibition Catalogue.

Jerome Mellquist and Lucie Wiese, *Paul Rosenfeld: Voyager in the Arts* (New York 1948).

Gorham Munson, " '291': A Creative Source of the Twenties," *Forum*, III (Fall-Winter 1960), 4-9.

Ward Muir, "Photographic Days," *The Amateur Photographer and Photography* (August 14, 1918).

Beaumont Newhall, "Stieglitz and '291,' " *Art in America*, LI, 1 (February 1963), 48-51.

Nancy Newhall, *Paul Strand; Photographs 1915-1945* (New York 1945).

Dorothy Norman, Waldo Frank, Lewis Mumford et al., *America and Alfred Stieglitz* (New York 1934).

Dorothy Norman, *Alfred Stieglitz: Introduction to an American Seer* (New York 1960). Published originally as an issue of *Aperture* (VIII, 1, 1960).

———, "Marin Speaks, and Stieglitz," *Magazine of Art*, XXX (March 1937), 151.

———, "Was Stieglitz a Dealer?" *Atlantic Monthly*, CLXXIX (May 1947), 22-23.

———, "Alfred Stieglitz on Photography," *The Magazine of Art*, XLIII (December 1950), 298-301.

———, "Stieglitz and Cartier-Bresson," *Saturday Review*, XLV (September 22, 1962), 52-56.

———, "Stieglitz's Experiments in Life," *New York Times Magazine* (December 29, 1963), 12-13.

Georgia O'Keeffe, "Stieglitz: His Pictures Collected Him," *New York Times Magazine* (December 11, 1949), 24-26 ff.

Daniel Catton Rich, *Georgia O'Keeffe* (Chicago 1943).

Andrew Carnduff Richie, *Charles Demuth* (New York 1959).

Paul Rosenfeld (Peter Minuit), "291," *The Seven Arts*, I (November 1916), 61-65.

Paul Rosenfeld, "Alfred Stieglitz," *The Dial*, LXX (April 1921), 397-409.

———, "American Painting," *The Dial*, LXXI, 6 (December 1921), 649-70.

Paul Rosenfeld, "The Watercolors of John Marin," *Vanity Fair*, xviii (April 1922), 48, 88, 92, 110.

———, "The Paintings of Marsden Hartley," *Vanity Fair*, xviii (August 1922), 47, 84, 94, 96.

———, "The Paintings of Georgia O'Keeffe," *Vanity Fair*, xix (October 1922), 56, 112, 114.

———, *Port of New York* (1924), intro. by Sherman Paul (Urbana 1961).

———, "Carl Sandburg and Photography," *The New Republic*, lxi (January 22, 1930), 251-53.

———, "After the O'Keeffe Show," *The Nation*, cxxxii (April 8, 1931), 388-89.

———, "Charles Demuth," *The Nation*, cxxxiii (October 7, 1931), 371-73.

———, "An Essay on Marin," *The Nation*, cxxxiv (January 27, 1932), 122-24.

———, "The Photography of Stieglitz," *The Nation*, cxxxiv (March 23, 1932), 350-51.

———, Alfred Stieglitz," *Twice a Year*, xiv-xv (1947), 203-05.

Herbert J. Seligmann, "A Photographer Challenges," *The Nation* (February 16, 1921), 268.

———, "Alfred Stieglitz and His Work at 291," *American Mercury*, ii (May 1924), 83-84.

———, *Alfred Stieglitz Talking; Notes on Some of his Conversations, 1925-1931* (New Haven 1966).

Alfred Stieglitz, "A Plea For a Photographic Art Exhibition," *The American Annual of Photography and Photographic Times Almanac* (1895), 27-28.

———, "The Progress of Pictorial Photography in the United States," *The American Annual of Photography and Photographic Times Almanac* (1899), 158-59.

———, "The Photo-Secession: Its Objects," *Camera Craft*, vii (August 1903), 81-83.

———, "Pictorial Photography," *Scribner's*, xxvi (November 1899), 528-37.

———, "Modern Pictorial Photography," *The Century Magazine*, lxiv (October 1902), 822-26.

Alfred Stieglitz, "The First Great Clinic to Revitalize Art," *New York American* (Sunday, January 26, 1913), 5-ce.

――――, "From the Writings and Conversations of Alfred Stieglitz," ed. Dorothy Norman, *Twice a Year*, I (Fall-Winter 1938), 77-110.

――――, "Ten Stories," ed. Dorothy Norman, *Twice a Year*, V-VI (1940-1941), 135-63.

――――, "Special Stieglitz Section," ed. Dorothy Norman, *Twice a Year*, VIII-IX (1942), 105-78.

――――, "Stories," ed. Dorothy Norman, *Twice a Year*, X-XI (1943), 245-64.

――――, "In Memoriam: Six Happenings (and a Conversation recorded by Dorothy Norman)," *Twice a Year*, XIV-XV (1947), 188-202.

G. Stone, "The Influence of Alfred Stieglitz on Modern Photographic Illustration," *American Photography*, XXX (April 1936), 199-206.

Paul Strand, "Photography," *The Seven Arts* (August 1917), 524-26.

――――, "Alfred Stieglitz and a Machine," *Manuscripts*, 2 (March 1922), 6-7.

――――, "Photography and the New God," *Broom*, III, 4 (November 1922), 252-58.

――――, "The Art Motive in Photography," *British Journal of Photography* (October 5, 1923), 612-15.

――――, "Georgia O'Keeffe," *Playboy*, 9 (July 1924), 16-20.

――――, "Stieglitz: An Appraisal," *Popular Photography*, XXI, 1 (July 1947), 62, 88-98. Includes a portfolio of Stieglitz's photographs.

J. J. Sweeney, "Rebel with a Camera," *New York Times Magazine* (June 8, 1947), 20-21, 41.

Horace Traubel, "Stieglitz," *Conservator*, XXVII, 10 (December 1916), 137.

Frederick S. Wight, *Arthur G. Dove* (Berkeley 1958).

Carl Zigrosser, "Alfred Stieglitz," *Twice a Year*, VIII-IX (Fall-Winter 1942), 137-45.

III. THE MAGAZINES OF THE NEW YORK AVANT GARDE

Camera Work, edited and published by Alfred Stieglitz (New York 1903-1917), 50 issues.

291, edited by Marius de Zayas and Agnes Ernst Meyer, published at 291 (New York, March 1915-February 1916), 12 issues.

Manuscripts, edited by Paul Rosenfeld (New York 1922-1923), 6 issues.

391, edited by Francis Picabia (25 January 1917-October 1924) 19 issues. Published in Barcelona, New York and Paris. Numbers 5 (June 1917), 6 (July 1917) and 7 (August 1917) were published in New York.

The Blind Man, edited by Marcel Duchamp (April-May 1917), 2 issues.

Rongwrong, edited by Marcel Duchamp (New York 1917), one issue.

New York Dada, edited by Marcel Duchamp (April 1921), one issue.

IV. GENERAL BACKGROUND

Conrad Aiken, *Scepticisms: Notes on Contemporary Poetry* (New York 1919).

Margaret Anderson, *My Thirty Years' War* (New York 1930).

Sherwood Anderson, *A Story Teller's Story* (New York 1924).

Guillaume Apollinaire, *Les Peintres Cubistes* (1913), ed. L. C. Breunig and J-Cl. Chevalier (Paris 1965).

"The Armory Show," *Art in America*, LI, 1 (February 1963), 24-64. Includes contributions by John Canaday, Bennard B. Perlman, Carl Zigrosser, Beaumont Newhall, William Carlos Williams, Doris Lane Butler, and Lloyd Goodrich.

John I. H. Baur, *Revolution and Tradition in Modern American Art* (Cambridge, Mass., 1951).

John Malcolm Brinnin, *The Third Rose* (New York 1959).

Milton W. Brown, *American Painting from the Armory Show to the Depression* (Princeton 1955).

———, *The Story of the Armory Show* (Greenwich, Conn. 1963).

Gabrielle Buffet-Picabia, *Aires Abstraites* (Geneva 1957).

Francis Carmody, "L'Esthétique de L'Esprit Nouveau," *Le Flâneur des Deux Rives*, II, 7-8 (December 1955).

Jean Cassou, Emile Langui, Nikolaus Pevsner, *Gateway to The Twentieth Century* (New York 1962).

Catalogue of the 50th Anniversary Exhibition of the Armory Show (New York 1963).

Henry Clifford, ed., *The Louise and Walter Arensberg Collection: Twentieth Century Section* (Philadelphia 1954).

Malcolm Cowley, *Exile's Return* (New York 1934).

Robert Delaunay, *Du Cubisme A L'Art Abstrait*, ed. Pierre Francastel (Paris 1957).

Bernard Dorival, *Twentieth Century Painters: Nabis, Fauves Cubists* (New York n.d.).

Katherine S. Dreier, *Western Art and the New Era* (New York 1923).

Marcel Duchamp, *Marchand du Sel* (Paris 1958).

Arthur J. Eddy, *Cubism and Post-Impressionism* (Chicago 1914).

Martin L. Friedman, *The Precisionist View in American Art* (Minneapolis 1960). Walker Art Center Exhibition Catalogue.

Henry Geldzahler, *American Painting in the 20th Century* (New York 1965).

Lloyd Goodrich, *Pioneers of Modern Art in America: The Decade of the Armory Show, 1910-1920* (New York 1963).

Lloyd Goodrich and John I. H. Baur, *American Art of the 20th Century* (New York 1961).

Christopher Gray, *Cubist Aesthetic Theories* (Baltimore 1953).

Guy Habasque, *Cubism* (Lausanne 1959).

SELECTIVE BIBLIOGRAPHY

Hutchins Hapgood, A Victorian in the Modern World (New York 1939).

Robert L. Herbert, ed., Modern Artists on Art (Englewood Cliffs 1964).

Marcel Jean, The History of Surrealist Painting (New York 1960).

Nicholas Joost, Scofield Thayer and the Dial (New York 1964).

Matthew Josephson, Life Among the Surrealists (New York 1962).

Wassily Kandinsky, Concerning the Spiritual in Art (1912) (New York 1947).

Wassily Kandinsky and Franz Marc, Der Blaue Reiter, ed. Klaus Lankheit (Munich 1965).

Alfred Kreymborg, Mushrooms (New York 1916).

———, Troubadour (New York 1925).

———, Our Singing Strength (New York 1929).

Walter Kuhn, The Story of the Armory Show (New York 1938).

Emile Langui, La Peinture Sous le Signe D'Apollinaire (Brussels 1950).

Oliver W. Larkin, Art and Life in America (New York 1949).

J. Nilsen Laurvik, Is it Art? (New York 1913).

Fernand Léger, Fonctions de la Peinture (Paris 1965).

Jean Lipman, ed., What Is American in American Art? (New York 1963).

Robert McAlmon, Being Geniuses Together, An Autobiography (London 1938).

Jerome Mellquist, The Emergence of an American Art (New York 1942).

Harriet Monroe, A Poet's Life (New York 1938).

Robert Motherwell, ed., The Dada Painters and Poets (New York 1951).

Gorham Munson, Destinations: A Canvas of American Literature Since 1900 (New York 1928).

Bernard S. Myers, Expressionism (London 1963).

208

Beaumont Newhall, "Photography as Art in America," *Perspectives*, 15 (Spring 1956), 122-33.

Beaumont and Nancy Newhall, *Masters of Photography* (New York 1958).

Ozenfant, *Foundations of Modern Art* (New York 1952). New, augmented edition.

Ezra Pound, *The Letters of Ezra Pound*, ed. D. D. Paige (New York 1950).

Man Ray, *Self Portrait* (New York 1963).

Hans Richter, *Dada—Kunst und Antikunst* (Cologne 1964).

James J. Rorimer, *The Unicorn Tapestries at the Cloisters* (New York 1962).

Michel Sanouillet, *Picabia* (Paris 1964).

Michel Seuphor, *Le Style et le Cri* (Paris 1965).

James Thrall Soby, *Juan Gris* (New York 1958).

Gertrude Stein, *The Autobiography of Alice B. Toklas* (New York 1933).

René Taupin, *L'Influence du Symbolisme Français sur la Poésie Américaine* (Paris 1929).

Joshua C. Taylor, *Futurism* (New York 1961).

Willy Verkauf, *Dada, Monographie einer Bewegung* (St. Gallen 1958).

William Wasserstrom, *The Time of the Dial* (Syracuse 1963).

Marius de Zayas and Paul B. Haviland, *A Study of the Modern Evolution of Plastic Expression* (New York 1913).

INDEX

Para Allyson